Tools for Change

Tools for Change

An invitation to dance

Becky Malby and Martin Fischer

Kingsham

First published in 2006
by Kingsham Press

Oldbury Complex
Marsh Lane
Easthampnett
Chichester, West Sussex
PO18 0JW
United Kingdom

Illustrations by Daria Martin

Typeset in Minion

Printed and bound by
Ashford Colour Press
Unit 600, Fareham Reach
Fareham Road
Gosport
Hants
UK

ISBN: 1-904235-55-7

British Library Cataloging in Publication Data
A catalogue record of this book is available from the British Library

Malby, Becky; Fischer, Martin

Contents

About the authors

We passionately believe that the ideas embedded in the theories of living systems explain how organisations really work and offer insights into how to intervene effectively in complex systems. We have been working with these ideas for many years, exploring the implications for leadership and for organisational processes, and experimenting with practices. Here we share what we have learnt. Our intent is to enhance your capacity and capability to intervene effectively in your own organisation.

This toolkit is aimed at anyone leading organisational change. For those of you commissioning organisational development, or putting in place OD processes, there are specific practices here that we hope you find useful.

Becky Malby is the Founder and Director of Complex Systems Associates Ltd, and an organisational and leadership Development Consultant. She has a track record in leadership development in the UK and Europe, and in whole systems development. She is the Director of the Centre for Innovation in Health Management at the University of Leeds.

Martin Fischer has a passion for inter-sectoral work using ideas of self-organising living systems. As well as working with organisations and whole systems, he also runs leadership development programmes at the Kings Fund, where he is a Senior Fellow. Martin has also been a member of "Inquiring Friends", an international group of cutting-edge practitioners in the field of living systems.

Acknowledgements

The origins of this work are conversations that took place at the self-organising systems seminars in the mid-1990s led by Margaret Wheatley and Myron Rogers, with Fritjof Capra; and the subsequent Inquiry Group at the Kings Fund. Over the years, we have been talking with and working with colleagues, particularly Margaret Wheatley, Myron Rogers and the Urban Partnership Group – Diane Plamping, Julian Pratt, Pat Gordon, who have guided our practice and helped shape our thinking. Much of this practice book comes from the synthesis of their ideas.

We offer our thanks to all our colleagues who contributed to our learning over the years, and also those that have offered their own designed practices here, particularly Juanita Brown, Julian Pratt, Myron Rogers, Robert Jacobs, Harrison Owen and Etienne Wenger. Additionally we are most grateful to Daria Martin for the chapter on strategic illustrations and would also like to offer our thanks to those who read through the many drafts and offered feedback.

Acknowledgements

An invitation to dance

This toolkit is really a beginning, and an invitation to dance. It's not the whole story, and we hope that if you do want to work and play with any of the ideas here, you will use the much more complete versions of the ideas and the practices detailed in the resources sections. If you have a go, or have previously used any of these ideas/practices and would like to add to what we have here (tips, better ways of doing it....), we would love to hear from you.

If you have any queries please email us:

becky.malby@complex-systems-ltd.co.uk or **mfischer@kingsfund.org.uk**

The beginning

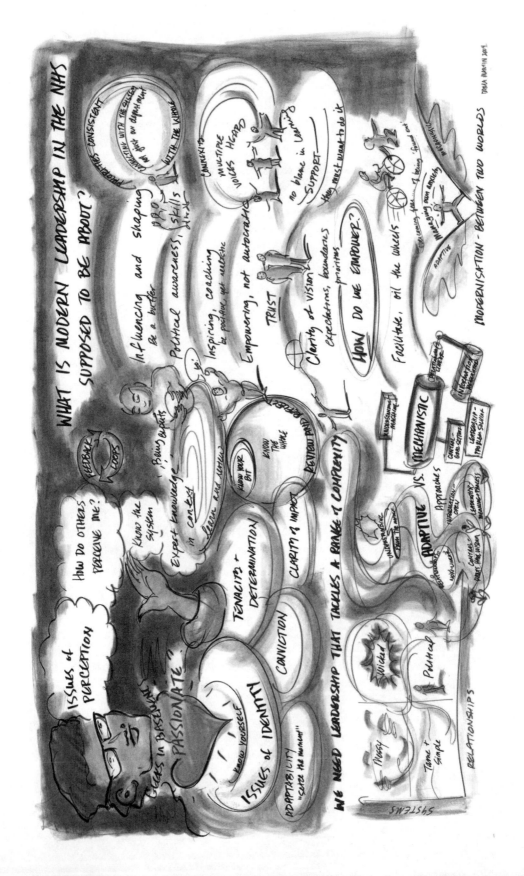

Wouldn't it be great if we were able to predict the impact of everything we did; if we knew that if we did X, Y would happen? Wouldn't it make our lives as leaders of change easy? The thing is, on the whole, life just isn't like that. We live our lives working through varying degrees of messiness, unknowability, unpredictability, surprises, anxiety, and excitement. Somewhere in all this we know that we have the power to make change, that the choices we have made in our lives have shaped how our world has turned out for us, and those around us.

We look back and see that sometimes what felt like the smallest choice at the time, has had huge implications, and what seemed monumentally difficult, has not had the impact we thought it would – and we are relieved! Lots of what we have done had intended and unintended consequences. But there is a pattern. We can see that the pattern of how we behave with others has shaped our relationships at work and home.

How strange that we persist in a model of working that says that the boss knows the answer, and the followers just have to follow their instructions for everything to work out as planned. We all know life isn't like that. As we begin to shape living things to suit us (genetic modification; the latest variety of tulip at the Chelsea Flower Show), we have found that actually there are some lessons in how living things work that could help us in our work. The lessons from living systems have been applied in many aspects of our world (go to a children's movie and you'll see the impact of learning about how birds flock when any computer-generated images work as a group – Batman; Star Wars).

Maybe there are lessons here for tackling messy, complex, multi-dimensional, unpredictable problems. We are not talking here about straightforward stuff where following the recipe gets you the result (payroll system; baking rock buns); or complicated stuff, where to solve the problem you need to break it down to constituent parts, engage experts, and work out what to do (building the channel tunnel) because the sum of the parts actually does make a whole. We are talking about complex issues (bringing up kids, improving the care of children with disabilities).

When we are in small teams trying to make a difference to a few people's lives (take a ward in a hospital) we talk about 'management', 'the system' and 'other professionals' as something that gets in the way of common sense. It is clear what to do to make the whole thing work better for the patients, but it's a mammoth task to get it to happen – the doctors don't want to change their routines; the management would need to talk to the unions to agree new terms and conditions for the nurses; the small amount of money you need doesn't fit into any of the hospital's defined budgets so you can't bid for it.

The authors started working with these ideas, because they just made sense to us. They appeared to be a much more real way of explaining the way people, teams, organisations, and systems actually work. The difficult part came when trying to work out what this meant in terms of our own behaviour. If we aren't going to do it the 'old' way, the one that everyone is familiar with, the world of business plans, Gant charts, humans as machines, oversimplification of complex issues, what way are we going to do it? Somehow, instinctively, we knew that we co-create the world we live in; that what you pay attention to shapes other's response (think back to clinical audit; performance management, and to the current targets); that we needed to be congruent between our beliefs, principles and behaviours. We liked looking for patterns and feedback loops. We liked trying to make sense of the context. So we were already working in ways that were congruent with these ideas. But in making the leap to understand the ideas in practice, we recognised some of the personal hurdles we, and others working with us, would have to make. For a start, working with these ideas means that you can't hide behind others – blaming them for things going wrong in your own lives! It means not hiding from difficulties and conflict, but surfacing them and working with them. It means things could get worse before they get better.

We got drawn into these ideas through stories – meeting people working with the ideas, telling their own stories about what happened. So let us tell you a few stories that might create a spark of interest in the rest of our offer here to you.

The bank

We were asked to go and see a MD working in a UK bank – the housing part. We turned up, and spent the first hour talking with the MD and his team. At the end we spent 10 minutes debriefing the session, giving each other feedback – the way they do in all their meetings and discussion groups. We were rather taken aback; whilst we espouse this practice, we had never experienced it as a core business process before.

We went onto a lunchtime discussion group, where anyone from the company can come to discuss ideas. This one was set up around a paper the MD had read about complex systems and had sent out to the whole workforce. A huge number of people were crammed into the room, from executive directors to secretaries, all wanting to give their views and listen to others. It was a highly participative, energetic and informed discussion. On the floor, everyone worked in self-managing teams, the MD didn't have an office, and he located himself where there was space. The result of this highly participative organisation, brimming with ideas, where people felt part of something worthwhile, was a significant improvement in performance.

Dumcree

The new District Commander for Craigavon in Northern Ireland charged with policing the Dumcree Sunday marches, took one look at the situation and knew that more of the same wasn't going to work. Over the previous years violence had escalated and continued days after the Sunday march. He decided to take a different approach, the crux of which was to confront the Orange Order and the Garvaghy Road residents with their responsibilities. Rather than escalating policing, he challenges the assumptions and norms that had led to huge barriers, heavy police presence, and escalating violence. He worked with his force and the army to identify the patterns that had emerged over the years, including their own behaviour. He did something very different, most symbolically by scaling down the physical barriers, and increasing surveillance. Now those that were intent on harm were identified quickly and charged quickly. Police were harmed at the bridge, but the ongoing violence was limited. The subsequent years have seen a much smaller demonstration, more orderly, more co-operative and violence has been dramatically reduced, as has the funding that the police need for Dumcree Sundays.

This book is for anyone wanting to make a real difference in their area of work, but tripping up on how to do it.

> "This old world was characterised by the need to manage *things* – stone, wood, iron.
> The new world is characterised by the need to manage complexity.
> Complexity is the very stuff of today's world."
>
> Stafford Beer (1975)

References

Beer, S. (1975) *Platform for Change*. Wiley, p. 380.

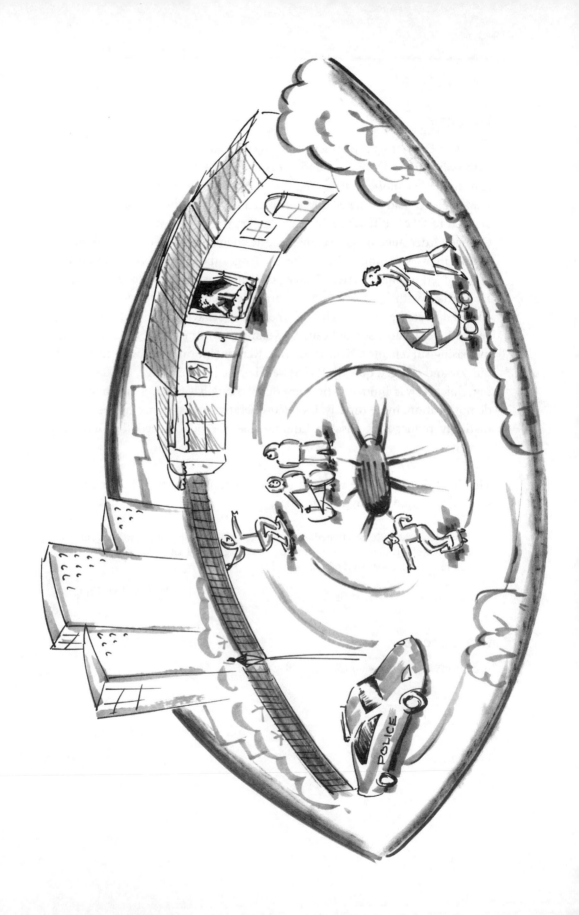

The ideas

Introduction

"If people are machines, seeking to control us makes sense, if we believe that there is no order to human activity except that imposed by the leader, that there is no self-regulation except that dictated by policies; if we believe that responsible leaders must have their hands into everything, controlling every decision, person and movement, then we cannot hope for anything except what we already have – a treadmill of frantic efforts that end up destroying our individual and collective vitality."

Margaret Wheatley (1999)

Systems theories have been evident in management and leadership practice for over 50 years. As the ideas and theories have developed, bringing together systems thinking from the fields of biology, physics, mathematics and ecology, so we have begun to see strands that inter-link. Here we give you an overview of the strands that build on the ideas first described in Fritjof Capra's *The Web of Life*, followed by a slightly longer explanation, and links to reference and reading material.

These ideas are then followed by some basic introduction about change in systems, and a set of practices that can help you in designing systems change. The practices cross-reference to the strands of the theory, and to the key lessons we have learnt about change in complex social systems.

In the theory pieces that follow we condense deep ideas into very short summaries. It is possible that this will confuse you rather than help you! If you are intrigued by our summaries, then please read the books and articles listed in the resources section at the end. The strands of theory that we weave together are:

Systems
- "A system is a perceived whole whose elements 'hang together' because they continually affect each other over time and operate towards a common purpose" (Senge, 2001)
- In complex systems cause and effect are distant in time and space – not immediate (Sternman, 2000).
- Order emerges for free – the system knows how to act. The system does what it is designed to do.
- The system looks different depending on where you are in it. To understand complex systems you need multiple perspectives from within the system.

- Complex social systems require clarity of expectations; congruency in decisions and actions; clear feedback mechanisms.

Emergence
- Simple dynamic rules give rise to extraordinarily intricate behaviours. Complex systems are full of surprises and unpredictability (Wheatley & Kellner-Rogers, 1996/7).
- They produce, through emergence, order that is diverse and spontaneous.
- The whole is different from the parts, and from the sum of the parts.
- Emergent properties are specific to the level of complexity, and are not evident at other levels i.e. emergent properties are not generic to the system.

Cognition
- What you see is what you get. – you do not understand what you see – you see what you understand.
- What you see determines what you do.
- "We bring forth the world" (Maturana & Varela, 1987).
- Communication is the co-ordination of behaviour (Maturana & Varela, 1987).
- Cognition is inseparable from emotion (Maturana & Varela, 1987).

Autopoiesis
- Systems seek to make and maintain themselves – they do nothing other than protect/conserve their identity.
- They are continually self-referencing.
- External events never determine responses in the system (Von Krogh & Roos, 1995).
- Identity is manifested in traditions, symbols, rituals, language, stories, practices (Gioia & Thomas, 1996).

Dissipative systems
- Complexity leads to order not disorder.
- Every path is unique – you can't tell how you got there, neither does it transfer.
- All living systems are hungry. The sources of energy include information, conflict and diversity (Wheatley, 1999).

Social systems
- The fundamental unit is the Social. Understanding does not come from understanding individual's behaviour, but from understanding the collective's behaviour (Dalal, 1998).
- Collective is the natural form.
- Social systems are drawn to possibilities not problem solving, and are self-aware.
- Systems exist only in language and communicative action (Anderson and Goolishian, 1988).
- Change occurs through conversations.
- Stories provide the lived experience.

The implications for leaders is that they need to:
- Contextualise – help the system make sense of the context in which it works.
- Be clear about purpose and expectations.
- Lead decisions that are congruent and consistent with this purpose.
- Connect the system to itself through dialogue and feedback processes, and help the system understand the impact of its actions.
- Find simple rules that enable the organisation to act.
- Question underlying assumptions that govern the system's action.

References

Anderson, H. & Goolishian, H. (1988) Human systems as linguistic systems: preliminary and evolving ideas about the implications for clinical theory. *Family Process*, **27**, pp 371–393.

Capra, F. (1997) *The Web of Life*. London: Flamingo.

Dalal, F. (1998) *Taking the Group Seriously. Towards and post-Foulkesian Group Analysis Theory*. London: Jessica Kingsley.

Gioia, D.A. & Thomas, J.B. (1996) Identity, image, and issue interpretation: sensemaking during strategic change in academia. *Administrative Science Quarterly*, **41**, pp.370–403.

Senge, P. (2001) *The Dance of Change. The Challenges of Sustaining Momentum in Learning Organizations*. London: Nicholas Brealey.

Sternman, J.D. (2000) *Business Dynamics: Systems Thinking and Modelling for a Complex World*. Boston: Irwin McGraw-Hill.

Maturana, H. & Varela, F.J. (1992) *The Tree of Knowledge. The Biological Roots of Human Understanding*. London: Shambhala.

Von Krogh, G. & Roos, J. (1995) *Organizational Epistemology*. London: Macmillan Press.

Wheatley, M. (1999) *Leadership and the New Science. Discovering Order in a Chaotic World*. San Francisco: Berrett-Koehler.

Wheatley, M. & Kellner-Rogers, M. (1996/7) *Self-organising Systems Seminars*. Sundance, USA. Unpublished.

Systems

The word 'System' is an integral part of our working every day language: it's a systems failure; the system isn't working; working the whole system. But the word itself represents a discipline of thought that has changed considerably over the last century. You might be familiar with force field analysis; open systems; process systems; Checkland's systems thinking. These are all completely different approaches to systems and don't travel into current thinking on complex systems. In the earlier approaches systems were boxes you could manipulate and control. This is fundamentally different from the ideas presented here. As more and more disciplines have become involved in exploring systems, from physicists, deep ecologists, mathematicians, to social scientists, a theory of living systems has emerged, and is still developing.

When you think about a system what comes to mind? Maybe in your house you would think of the electrical system. You know that this has a direct cause and effect relationship. You press your light switch, the light comes on. Predictable, orderly, knowable. This is a mechanistic system. It is completely appropriate where it is absolutely known that when you do A, B happens and nothing else.

Maybe you would think of your family as a system. Now here is a minefield of unpredictability. Whilst there are patterns of relationships in the family, and a strong identity, doing A does not predict that B will definitely happen (just think teenage children). Moreover, if you do A, if B does happen, then so does lots else (C, D, E and F!). These are the unintended, unpredictable, consequences of doing A. Some of these might be OK, others are just really difficult. These are complex adaptive systems. This is the territory of this book – the complex not the complicated.

> **Cause and effect in complex systems**
> 1. Our decisions have multiple consequences
> 2. Our decisions change the environment, influencing the decisions of others
> 3. The multiple consequences of our decisions are often delayed.
>
> In complex systems, cause and effect are distant in time and space (Sternman, 2000).

One of the phrases that seems to resonate and have found a way into organisational language is: 'The whole is more than the sum of its parts'. You can know nothing about wetness by knowing everything there is to know about hydrogen and oxygen. Originally it was thought that by understanding the relationships between the parts of a system, we could understand the system and predict its behaviour. We now know that every system has its own systemic emergent properties (i.e they only show up in that level of system) that are properties only of the whole; they are not present in the parts. In effect there are no parts, just systems within systems. Each system has its own unique properties and identity. We feel that the whole is actually different from the parts.

> "The greatest shock to scientists in the 20th century was the realisation that you can understand nothing, absolutely nothing, about the whole by understanding the parts."
>
> Fritjof Capra (1997)

> "A system is a perceived whole whose elements 'hang together' because they continually affect each other over time and operate towards a common purpose (tightly interconnected)."
>
> Peter Senge (2001)

Understanding systems requires us to develop the rigour of contextualisation (exploring the context and our understanding of its actual and possible impact on the system). The system operates in the context of systems it is part of and other systems that are part of it. It is the pattern of relationships within a system and between systems that matter. By spending time developing and understanding the relationships in a system, and by uncovering the multiple perspectives that are held by players in the system, you can reach far more possibilities from which to choose action. The system itself has the capacity and insights to know what to do.

In this view of systems thinking, order emerges for free under the necessary conditions. Systems all have a set of principles which govern how they operate. These are embedded in the system's structure. Here we use 'structure' and 'organisation' with a very particular meaning.

Structure
What the system is made of + the way the pattern of organisation is embedded.

Organisation

The relationships and connections between its parts.

Fritjof Capra (1997)

Examples, therefore, of 'elements of structure in an organisation' are not the usual hierarchical charts, but the following:

* Physical layout and environment.
* Information flows.
* Policies and procedures.
* Practices and norms.
* Reporting relationships.
* Reward systems.
* Performance measures.
* Language.

Thus complex adaptive/social systems self-organise around the known and enacted principles and structure. The system knows how to act. However, this does not leave leaders feeling powerful in the traditional way. Operating from a persistent drive to understand the systems purpose, and consistently and congruently operationalising agreed principles, and embedding these in structure (see above), is not how most of us articulate leadership. Systems do not require managers and leaders to determine roles, give instructions, dish out tasks, and expect people to do exactly as they say. As we know, if we do A, B does not necessarily happen, and if it does, so does a lot else. Complex systems require leaders to have clarity of expectations; congruency in decisions and actions; clear feedback mechanisms. There is no one systems organiser. Operating under the illusion that managers and leaders can control complex adaptive or social systems as an act of powerful will and grip, is an inhibitor to system's performance, not an enabler.

References, reading and resources

Capra, F. (1997) *The Web of Life*. London: Flamingo.

Senge, P. (2001) *The Dance of Change. The Challenges of Sustaining Momentum in Learning Organizations*. London: Nicholas Brealey.

Sternman, J.D. (2000) *Business Dynamics: Systems Thinking and Modeling for a Complex World*. Boston: Irwin McGraw-Hill.

Wheatley, M. (1999) *Leadership and the New Science. Discovering Order in a Chaotic World*. San Francisco: Berrett-Koehler.

Emergence

"Systems unique capabilities for novelty, learning and communication come about not by way of design but through emergence."

Fritjof Capra (1997)

Complex systems are full of surprises and unpredictability. These systems produce, through emergence, order that is diverse and spontaneous. In complex social systems, bringing together people to have conversations and discover new and different ways of doing things, brings about more order than project plans ever will. When we write strategies with actions and timescales, we know that these are more expressions of desired intent than any resemblance of what will actually happen. This is not a call to just let anything happen, but a quest for the simple organising rules of thumb that enable the emergent properties of a system to come into being.

Linear cause and effect models (the basis for most of our planning) assume that:

1. The environment can be simplified enough to be modelled into a limited number of variables.
2. The environment will stay constant such that the variables stay the same.
3. The system will be predictable in how it reacts to these variables, no matter what the feedback loops are telling it, no matter what is going on internally.

Faucheux and Makaridakis (1979)

In complex social systems this is obviously not so.

Complexity is where a great many independent agents are interacting with each other in a great many ways, where very simple dynamic rules can give rise to extraordinary intricate behaviour. We can't plan for emergence; there are no 'levers' to be pulled. There are some conditions that support it. One of these is the discovery of simple rules to govern behaviour. All organisations have rules/guiding principles/rules of thumb, that can be both helpful and unhelpful.

An example of some rules that produce co-ordinated behaviour are those that simulate birds flocking (Boids) created by Craig Reynolds. It turns out that you only need 3 rules:

1. Each boid tries to maintain a minimum distance from other objects in the environment, including other boids.
2. Each boid tries to maintain the same speed as the other boids in its neighbourhood.
3. Each boid tries to move towards the perceived centre of the mass of boids in its neighbourhood.

Note:

- There are no rules about forming a flock;
- The rules were entirely local, referring only to what an individual boid could see and do in its own vicinity;
- If a flock forms, it does so from the bottom up, as an emergent phenomenon.

To see this in action go to http://www.red3d.com/cwr/boids/applet/. Another example of using simple rules to reach very different behaviours can be seen at http://www.icosystem.com/game.htm.

So let's explore what 'rules of thumb' or 'guiding principles' are. Well, we all work with 'beliefs', usually embedded in 'visions' statements. These beliefs in themselves don't necessarily help you decide what to do in any situation you are faced with in your organisational life. The next step is to create a set of principles from these beliefs that actually guide you when choosing how to act on a day-to-day basis.

Some examples of simple rules of thumb

(Note these cover a range of levels of complexity/system.)

1. This is an example from a group of leaders of organisations within a Strategic Health Authority

> **We speak well of each other**
> Differences of view around the table are encouraged and debated when decisions are made. There is then no place for undermining comments to other audiences.

2. This is an example of a rule developed as part of guidance for delivering appropriate services for all – produced from the experiences of black and ethnic minority groups.

> **Organisations need feedback mechanisms to link the individual and the organisational learning.**

3. The belief that underpins this next 'rule of thumb' is that a colour and colour blind approach suggests prejudice.

> **Ask, do note assume. Asking is a sign of respect.**
> Not knowing is not being unprofessional. Assuming is. Simply acknowledging a person's difference and asking is not in itself racist or discriminatory.

4. A rule of thumb that emerged as part of a strategy for 'going home from hospital'.

> **If in doubt, ask the patient and carer.**

Pratt, Plamping et al (1998)

5. This rule of thumb was developed for a strategy event lead by a local authority:

> **Participation matters**
> - Everyone has a role in making their voice heard and in listening to others' views/opinions.
> - If we disagree or dissent, then we do this in a supportive, thoughtful way.
> - We can only move forward if we challenge what we don't believe or agree with.
> - We need to be respectful and mindful of views different from our own.

Other conditions that support emergence are:

1. The connectivity of the system and the ability to hear diversity of views and multiple perspectives.
2. Open access to information.
3. Manage anxiety (yours and others) so that old ways of doing things don't reappear.
4. Clear boundaries for the work, including clear intent.
5. Patience – not leaping to action too soon, taking time to see the patterns that emerge.

References, reading and resources

Faucheux C & Makridakis S. (1979) Automation or autonomy in organizational design. *International Journal General Systems*, 5, pp. 213–220.

Kauffman, S. (1996) *At Home in the Universe: The Search for Laws of Self-Organization and Complexity*. Oxford University Press.

Peterson, C. & Pergamit, G. (1997) *Leaping the Abyss: Putting Group Genius to Work*. Knowhere Press.

Pratt, J., Plamping, D., Ombler-Spain, S., Harries, J., Gordon, P., Fischer, M. & Evans, K. (1998) The NHS – order for free? Proceedings from the Organisations as Complex Systems Conference, Warwick.

Wheatley, M. & Kellner-Rogers, M. (1996) *A Simpler Way*. San Francisco: Berrett-Koehler.

http://www.red3d.com/cwr/boids/applet/

http://www.icosystem.com/game.htm.

Cognition

"The real voyage of discovery consists not in seeing new landscapes,
but in having new eyes"

Proust

What you see is what you get. What you see determines what you do

We were taught in school that we 'see' a tree by the impact of light waves on the back of the retina (remember the pictures of the tree and the eyeball, with the tree becoming an upside down picture on the back of your eye?). It turns out that actually we form pictures only partly through the impact of light waves. Many more stimuli, including previous experience and memory, all contribute to what we see. Moreover what we see is entirely internally generated. External stimuli only perturb us. We decide internally which of these external stimuli to notice, and how to interpret them. This theoretical position (Maturana and Varela 1992) transforms our understanding of cognition. Simply – we bring forth the world. External events never determine responses in the system; at the most they trigger structure-determined reactions.

Cognition is the process by which autopoietic systems make and maintain themselves. Cognition is an integral part of the way a living organism interacts with its environment. It does not react to environmental stimuli through a linear chain of cause and effect, but responds with structural changes in its non-linear, organisationally closed network. This type of response enables the organism to continue living in its environment. In other words, the organism's cognitive interaction with its environment is intelligent interaction. From the perspective of Santiago theory, intelligence is manifest in the richness and flexibility of an organism's structural coupling.

Perturbations (disturbances, triggers) from the environment trigger structural changes in the system. The network of components in the system respond to these perturbations by rearranging their pattern of connections. The system specifies its own structural change, and which perturbations from the environment trigger these changes. A system brings forth its own world. It is only through recurrent interactions that the system adapts and learns. The environment never specifies the system's change in its identity, it only triggers that change. Each system builds its own distinctive world.

Inherently we probably know this. We only have to talk with our friends to see that we all interpret the same action in the world differently, be it from a letter coming home from school about changes to the school day; or how much pocket money to give! In our organisations when we join we always look for both 'how things are done round here' and how the organisation interprets what is going on in the wider system, be it the importance of a specific policy; the relationship it has with its partners; how it sees its users, etc. The same policy, the same expression of need by users triggers very different responses in different organisations. In terms of a policy, this can be a complete reorganisation of priorities around that policy, or a complete disregard of it, in two neighbouring organisations.

According to Santiago theory, cognition is not a representation of an independent, pre-given world, but rather a bringing forth of a world. What is brought forth by a particular organism in the process of living is not *THE* world but *A* world, one that is always dependent upon the organism's structure.

The system is triggered, or not, by data from the environment depending on its own internal structure. It interprets this data using its own way of seeing, its lens (identity), and determines if this data, as interpreted, requires action. It takes action and then looks for feedback about the impact of that action. This means also that the system gets more of whatever it pays attention to. Some organisations seem 'blind' to certain environmental triggers. For instance, NHS organisations that have no performance measures or commissioning strategy specifically for elderly people, even though this group is the highest proportion of service users. It has been fascinating that in looking at Accident and Emergency admissions, hospitals have suddenly come to realise that a small group of elderly people are coming through their doors on a very regular basis. It has only been by paying attention to patterns of A&E admissions, that service solutions are being provided that intervene with this group well before they get to A&E. It just wasn't a problem that the system had seen.

Moreover systems exist only in language and communicative action (Maturana & Varela, 1992) in that it is only in conversing that:

- We determine what the system is – who we talk to – who is included.
- We determine the system's identity – stories of how things are done round here.
- We co-ordinate our action, checking our understanding of what to do.

You may have been in a meeting, agreed an action, and be surprised to see how others have interpreted that action/agreement. You think that the decision was clear and apparent to everyone. The same words hold different meanings for different people – it's all in cognition! We all have different understandings of the same words; you only have to see a teenager sitting love-struck by the phone waiting for the call from the idol who said 'see you later'!

"Communication is the co-ordination of behaviour, not the transmission of information."

Maturana & Varela (1992)

We must call into question the idea that the world is pre-given, and that cognition is representation. In cognitive science, this means that we must call into question the idea that information exists ready-made in the world and that it is extracted by a cognitive system.

Finally, cognition is inseparable from emotion. A new marketing strategy by a neighbouring competitor could be interpreted as aggressive. This could mean that your system responds aggressively itself. It could also be interpreted as exciting, a new initiative that triggers creativity in your own system. It could create anxiety. In your own body you know that emotions take on physical characteristics (anxiety is detected by heightened colour, faster pulse, restlessness). All cognition has an associated emotional response. This in turn is inseparable from the social domain (language, thought). In working through how the system 'sees' the world, its emotional response is one indicator, which is usually accessed through stories being told about what's going on (see social systems).

References, reading and resources

Maturana, H. and Varela, F.J. (1992) *The Tree of Knowledge. The Biological Roots of Human Understanding.* London: Shambhala.

Weick, K.E. (1995) *Sensemaking in Organizations.* London: Sage Publications.

Bortoft, H. (1996) *The Wholeness of Nature. Goethe's Way Toward a Science of Conscious Participation in Nature.* New York: Lindisfarne Press.

Self-making (autopoietic) systems

The word for self- making, or self-producing is 'autopoiesis'. The product of an autopoietic system is itself. All living systems are autopoietic. It is our proposition that this is also the case for complex social systems.

Living systems make and maintain themselves (e.g. humans – we start as a single cell and make all our blood, bones, organs). As we explored in the section on cognition, a living system itself both specifies what in the world it notices and how it responds (what perturbs it and how it will react to the perturbance). They do nothing other than protect/conserve their identity. All identities are changeable over time.

Identity matters because it is the boundary for all action in a system.

A living system generates its own components, which in turn generates the whole. The system is defined by its identity; it is physically defined by its boundaries. The structure of the system[1] (what the system is made of + the way the pattern of organisation is embedded e.g. physical environment, reporting relationships, policies and procedures, reward systems, performance metrics) may change over time, but the organisation (the relationship and connections between its parts) remains the same. Not only do these systems produce themselves; they are also continually self-referring, so that perception of reality is created internally, not externally.

Not only do these systems produce themselves; they are also continually self-referring, so that perception of reality is created internally not externally.

Autopoietic systems:
- Are self-producing and autonomous
- Physically define themselves through the production of their boundaries.
- Are a network of components.
- Are simultaneously closed (it demarcates itself off from the rest of the world, clearly specifying what belongs to it from what does not) and structurally open.
- Are structurally determined – it is the particular structural relations at each moment in time that determine both what can influence or affect the system, and what the response will be.
- Are structurally coupled to their environment, they co-exist.
- Are self-referencing.

Von Krogh & Roos (1995)

---

[1] For fuller explanation see section on Systems.

In other words, all autopoietic systems:

*   use past experience and 'the way things are done round here – the way we go about this' to determine how to act;
*   do that within the limits of what they classify as 'our business';
*   in acting change the environment and change in response to the environment.

External events never *determine* responses in the system, but at the most *trigger* structure-determined reactions.

Identity, then is another essential condition for organisation. It is the self of the system that compels it toward particular actions and behaviours. It is the self that defines meaning. It is the self that invites people to change or compels them to resist.

> "Individuals come and go, but organisations preserve knowledge, behaviours, norms and values over time."
>
> Daft and Weick (1994)

If we think about people through time, then there is a similar puzzle. From our birth we are continually changing and developing. All the cells in our body change within a seven-year cycle so we are literally not the people we were. We constantly go through new situations and experiences. Yet, we remain remarkably consistent, presenting a similar "face" to the world over long periods of time.

> These dynamics occur not just at the level of the individual but also at the level of the social organisation. Many organisations have very strong senses of identity (e.g., the Scout Movement, the NHS, IBM, The Body Shop, the catholic religion, the MCC) that persist and endure over long periods of time, and despite major changes in their internal structure and external environment. How is it that an organisation can completely restructure and change many personnel, and yet still be experienced, internally and externally, as having an ongoing coherence? Equally, organisations might be thought to be fairly mechanistic, transforming inputs into products or services, and reacting deterministically to external pressures. In practice, however, organisations' responses are often far from predictable. A letter of complaint may generate a significant response from one organisation and none from another, or different responses at different times; strong reactions may be elicited simply by the use of particular key factors in a communication; repeated change management initiatives may well result in little substantive change.
>
> John Mingers (1995)

A system's identity:

- Is the system's distinctive character
- Is the 'product' of the system
- Is reflected in values manifested in traditions, symbols, and practices.
- Can be evidenced through the lens through which the system filters data and makes sense of that data.
- Is created through language and communication; reflection and dialogue; and is reinforced through organisation and structure.

Coherent organisations experience the world with less threat and more freedom. They don't create boundaries to defend and preserve themselves. They don't have to keep others out. Clear at their core, they become less and less concerned about where they stop. Inner clarity gives them expansionary range.

References, reading and resources

Daft, R.L. & Weick, K.E. (1984) Towards a model of organizations as interpretation systems. *Academy of Management Review*, 9, 2, pp. 284–295.

Maturana, H. and Varela, F.J. (1992) *The Tree of Knowledge. The Biological Roots of Human Understanding*. London: Shambhala.

Mingers, J. (1995) *Self-Producing Systems: Implications and Applications of Autopoiesis (Contemporary Systems Thinking)*. Plenum.

Von Krogh, G. & Roos, J. (1995) *Organizational Epistemology*. London: Macmillan Press.

Dissipative systems

Scientists have noticed that in seemingly mysterious ways, living forms combine stability of structure with fluidity of change (e.g. water going down a plug hole). Living organisms are characterised by continual flow and change in its metabolism – thousands of chemical reactions. Chemical and thermal equilibrium equals death.

The second law of thermodynamics – the trend in physical phenomena from order to disorder, is the classic way of seeing the world – a place of ever-increasing disorder as the natural state, which requires us to impose order to survive.

Prigogine (1981) wanted to solve the puzzle of order and dissipation (structure and change) and in his theory of dissipative structures finds that systems far from equilibrium, where there are multiple feedback loops and non-linearity, produce order for free. These systems have a greater number of solutions within them, choose paths based on feedback and on fluctuations sometimes very small – called noise) and quickly get to order of structure alongside fluidity of change.

Kauffman was interested in exploring how the complex network of human genes had developed, but he used light bulbs to demonstrate that self-organisation is a fundamental process found everywhere. He wired together a network of two hundred light bulbs. Each bulb was assigned a relationship with two other bulbs. It was to turn on or turn off based only on the behaviour of either of its assigned partners. Even with such simple conditions, the number of possible states of on–off bulbs is 10^{30}. The human imagination cannot begin to comprehend this number of possibilities. Yet Kauffman believed that the network would settle into a repeated state – a pattern of on–off bulbs. However, given such an astronomical number of possibilities, he expected to wait a long time before a pattern of behaviour emerged.

But the pattern of organisation appeared instantly. After exploring only thirteen states, the system of bulbs settled into a repeatable pattern, flashing on and off in a repetitive cycle of four configurations. With a universe of possibilities to explore, the bulbs organised immediately into four patterns. Even when the connections were changed, linking bulbs to two different partners, patterns emerged, new in design, but still patterns. Organisation always emerged instantly.

So, rather than complexity leading to disorder, it leads to order. The living world unfolds in increasing order and complexity.

We live in a universe where we get 'order for free'

Kauffman (1996)

Being off-equilibrium requires the system to take in energy.

In social systems this leads us to propose that:

1. All social systems are dissipative structures – open systems that maintain themselves far from equilibrium.
2. Every path is unique – you can't tell how you got there, neither does it transfer.
3. At the edge of chaos where there is increased complexity, order emerges.
4. All living systems are hungry. Some sources of energy in social systems are information, conflict and diversity – it creates the noise/feedback to enable the system to choose its path.

Information

Information – is data interpreted. In sharing perceptions of what data are showing us about the organisation/our team/the work, we get into conversations about identity, meaning and diverse perspectives. These conversations enable participants in them to shape their understanding of the system's purpose, identity, behaviours, and to contribute to those. Discussions about the meaning of data help players in the system co-ordinate their behaviour. Information energises a system by itself being the catalyst of meaning-making conversations.

Conflict

Conflict – or active pursuit of differences, is often seen as energy sapping, or energy wasting, not energy giving. Conflict is typically approached as an organisational problem – we look for consensus, collaboration, and sameness to indicate all is going well. Conflict pushes us to areas of discomfort. However, in systems, conflict – or active difference – is where new possibilities are generated, where the organisation's identity is truly discovered. Conflict tends to be rooted in differences of understanding, perception, and identity. It's not about right and wrong. We need to be able to get beyond closing down conflict, to authentic exploration of these differences in order to find new possibilities for action.

Contradictions appearing as differences of perception and value, normally involving debate and even tendencies to conflict, can be contained and made the occasion for mutual learning and respect

Funtowicz & Ravetz (1994, p. 578)

Basically conflict makes us think about our own position, and its usefulness.

Pairs of opposites .... put tension in the world, a tension that sharpens our sensitivity and increases our self-awareness.

Schumacher (1999)

For conflict to be energy giving, opposing parties need to explicate their position, and listen generously to their opponent's position. Both are valid as opinion is a construct of perspective and all perspectives are needed in order for the system to choose action.

To move from a condition of conflicting ideologies to an ecology of consciousness ...an ecology of associated differences...from mindless, passionate conflict to mindful dispassionate opposition.

Thompson (1998)

The trick here is to recognise the emotional aspect of conflict and determine a process that lives in respectful difference, and the commitment to work with differences to find a productive possibility.

Diversity

Stability is found in freedom – not in conformity and compliance. ... But sameness is not stability. It is individual freedom that creates stable systems. It is differentness that enables us to thrive.

Wheatley & Kellner-Rogers (1996)

Making the most of multiple perspectives is a critical condition for living systems. It is diversity that creates options. Often in organisations we see the noisy teams, the ones that persist in 'bucking the system' or challenging limitations, as difficult ones to manage. Actually they are the organisation's lifeblood. It is the noisy ones, the ones that stir things up, that help the organisation adapt. Taking time organisationally to look for the noise, for the different non-conforming voices, is an act of leadership.

References, reading and resources

Funcowicz, S. & Ravetz, J. (1994) Emergent complex systems. *Futures*, **26**, 6, pp. 568–582.

Gell-Mann, M. (1995) *The Quark and the Jaguar. Adventures in the Simple and the Complex*. London: Abacus.

Kauffman, S. (1996) *At Home in the Universe: The Search for Laws of Self-Organization and Complexity*. Oxford University Press.

Nonaka, I. (1995) *The Knowledge-Creating Company: How Japanese Companies Create the Dynamics of Innovation*. Oxford University Press.

Prigogine, I. (1984) Order out of chaos. In: Livingston, P. (ed.) Proceedings of the Stanford International Symposium. Stanford Literature Series. Anma Libri.

Schumacher, E.F. (1999) *Small Is Beautiful: Economics as if People Mattered: 25 Years Later ... with Commentaries*. Hartley & Marks.

Thompson, W.I. (1998) *Coming into Being: Artifacts and Texts in the Evolution of Consciousness*. Palgrave MacMillan.

Wheatley, M. & Kellner-Rogers, M. (1996) *A Simpler Way*. San Francisco: Berrett-Koehler.

Social systems

Why do we behave the way we do in groups and in organisations? So far we have been exploring scientific basis to complex adaptive systems drawing on the fields of mathematics, chemistry, physics, biology and deep ecology. The temptation is to use the complex adaptive system theory as a metaphor for how organisations work. We believe that CAS explains why organisations work the way they do. We believe that social systems are complex adaptive systems. But in social systems cells are not replaced by individuals – social systems do not reproduce individuals. So what is it that social systems reproduce? Social systems are primarily meaning-using systems that use communication (the co-ordination of behaviour through language and reflection) as the means of reproduction. So what is it that is particular and distinctive about human social systems? The distinction is the capacity for language and for reflexivity or self-awareness. The social system can be mapped in terms of social relatedness, i.e. the degree to which agents connect to form meaning. It is this meaning-making that enables individuals to change their own behaviour and to change the behaviour of others for collective purpose. Here we see the individual as both forming the collective, and being formed by the collective.

Culture (i.e. how individuals behave together in organisations) is an emergent phenomena of the interaction of the feedback loops between information, relationships, and identity. This means that understanding how individuals behave will not help us understand how groups/teams/organisations behave. The collective is a completely different unit than the individual, and it is the *only* unit in social systems.

What we know about communication is that it has both rational and affective components; every communication has an emotional response. Engaging with social systems requires us to focus on:

• Reflective, connected, sense-making conversations.
• Valuing both the affective and the rational.

Social systems are also drawn to possibility, to future, and are energised through what can be and what is, rather than what should have been. All too often in systems we concentrate on trying to solve problems. Meetings are all about what's not working. Reframing this to focusing on what does work (as proposed in appreciative inquiry) means making the most of what works; amplifying it; understanding the conditions that support what works; and concentrating on improving those conditions. It changes the question from 'What doesn't work here and how can we fix it?' to 'What works and how can we do more of it?'.

All of this is grounded in real-lived experience (hence the power of stories in organisations). In social systems stories are to transformation what facts are to science; they are the solid ground on which meaning is created. Abstract thought is the least powerful (although highly sophisticated) way to engage.

> Change occurs through conversations. Inquiry is about change. The seeds of change are implicit in the first questions we ask. Change is the evolution of new meaning through dialogue.
>
> Anderson & Goolishian (1998)

What does that mean for how we understand and intervene in social systems?

At an organisational level there are a number of assumptions:

- In every society, organisation, or group, something works.
- Organisational life is drawn to possibilities not to problem solving.
- What we focus on becomes our reality (see section on Cognition).
- Reality is created in the moment, and there are multiple realities.
- The act of asking questions of an organisation or group influences the group in some way.
- Identity is transmitted and shaped by stories.

What sort of conversations are reflexive conversations (ones that promote self-awareness)? A model of a reflective, connected conversation is receiver-based communication, where you:

- Start by listening
- Establish a process-response
- Tune the communication
- Develop a consistent alternative model

Social systems are formed and enacted in language and communication. This is the focus for our work here – finding ways to access the social system through questions, conversations, and sense-making.

References, reading and resources

Anderson, H. & Goolishian, H. (1988) Human systems as linguistic systems: Preliminary and evolving ideas about the implications for clinical theory. *Family Process*, **27**, pp. 371–393.

Cooperrider, D., Sorensen, P., Whitney, D. & Yaeger, T. (1999) *Appreciative Inquiry. Rethinking Human Organization Toward A Positive Theory of Change*. Stripes

Luhmann, N. (1995) *Social Systems*. Stanford: Stanford University Press.

Dalal, F. (1998) *Taking the Group Seriously*. London: Jessica Kingsley.

Application to organisations

Mechanistic or adaptive systems approach

As we said in the introduction, we are offering practices to work with complex systems. These systems are adaptive. Our day-to-day experience in organisations is primarily of working with mechanistic approaches, i.e. approaches designed to work in mechanistic systems. These systems are predictable i.e. when you do A, B always happens and nothing else. However, we find that the mechanistic way of understanding and working in systems (reductionist; problem-based; seeking predictable change; controlling information on a need to know basis) is being applied to complex systems inappropriately. Here is a summary of the difference between mechanistic and adaptive systems.

	Mechanistic	Adaptive
Understanding	Sum of the parts	Only comes from the whole
Cause and effect	Linear. Predictable	Distant in time and space. Non-linear. Intended and unintended consequences
Relationships	Based on requirements	Critical for possibility. Dependent on feedback. Reciprocity
Connectivity	Connection between components is fixed	Components dispersed and free to interact locally within a hierarchy
Behaviour	Controlled through directions. Simple/predictable	Emergent through guiding principles. Order for free
Capacity	Maximum, no waste	Redundant (i.e spare) capacity to adapt
Energy	Extrinsic	Intrinsic
Relationship with environment	Reacts to	Co-exists with
Boundaries	Set by design	Created through meaning
Information	Regulated	Open
Conflict and diversity	Discouraged and threatening	Encouraged through dialogue

What this means for looking at organisations

When looking at organisations in terms of their capacity as complex adaptive systems, what do these ideas suggest that we need to look for? Here are a number of areas that you would focus on:

- Identity – clear identity evident throughout the system. Evidenced in 'system' stories; common language; clarity of vision and purpose and member's identification with those in practice.
- Clarity of direction and how the system works to get there.
- Multiple perspectives encouraged and valued. Conflict seen as creative. Difference nurtured where it is creative.
- Clear, accessible, understood, used, and current principles for how things are done round here (rules of thumb).
- Open access to information.
- The systems seek and use feedback about its impact internally and externally.
- Reflexive – spends time in conversations for understanding, possibility and change. Looks for patterns of system behaviour.
- Boundaries clear for all members, and clarity in expectations, responsibility and accountability of members and of the whole.
- Sustainability – looks for change in the long term. Manages anxiety about the time for change, and things looking worse in the middle.
- Effective mature relationships across the organisation.

What this means for leadership

Working with these ideas shifts systems leaders away from the need to control and fix the system.

These ideas suggest that leaders of dynamic systems are required to:

- Provide **clarity of purpose and expectations**, leading from ambiguity and managing personal and system anxiety.

- Lead decisions that are **congruent and consistent** with this purpose and the articulated values of the system. This congruence is found in the **simple rules** used to govern the system (provide the framework for action and for holding players in the system to account) and the structure (what gets rewarded etc – see section on Systems).

- Be clear about the system's **boundaries and the expectations** of the whole systems and individual member's performance and behaviour. Clearly articulated responsibilities and accountability processes.

- **Contextualise** – help the system make sense of the context in which it works. This includes spotting patterns in both the external world and within the system itself (the trends over time in how the system acts). This also includes seeing options all the way through, working all the time with multiple scenarios.

- **Question underlying assumptions** that govern the system's actions – in effect persistently question the sense the system makes of data it gathers from the external world and from its internal workings. This includes surfacing **patterns**. In doing so, the systems leader can ask how the system's assumptions help and/or hinder its work, and uncover the systems' underlying operating principles (simple rules above).

- Systems leaders connect the system to itself through dialogue and feedback processes.

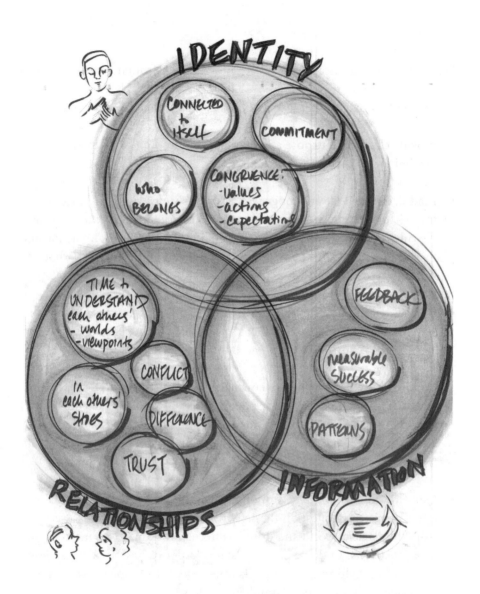

- Systems leaders need to sustain processes that enable the system to make the most of its capacity and capability to adapt. In essence this requires persistent attention to identity, relationships and information (Wheatley & Rogers, 1996).

Culture is an emergent property of the interaction between:

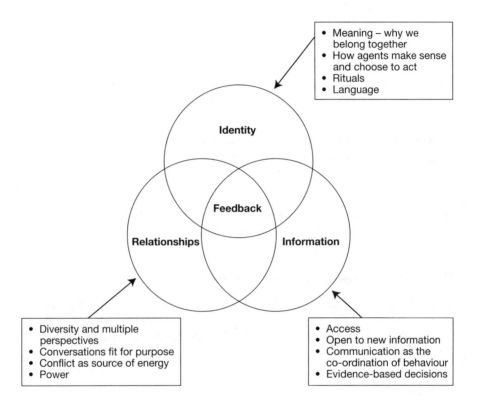

Meaning – why we belong together
- How agents make sense and choose to act
- Rituals
- Language

Identity

Feedback

Relationships

Information

- Diversity and multiple perspectives
- Conversations fit for purpose
- Conflict as source of energy
- Power

- Access
- Open to new information
- Communication as the co-ordination of behaviour
- Evidence-based decisions

When asked what counts as 'success' or 'is the system working?' many boards and executive teams find it difficult to articulate together what success looks like for the whole organisation, or even if the system is working as a whole. It is this clarity that is required of systems leaders. Clarity about what 'it is working' looks like helps define what leaders pay attention to for feedback. Feedback itself is a systems intervention. You get more of what you pay attention to. So relying only on externally set expectations does not necessarily in itself help the system organise effectively. There are multiple ways of achieving short-term goals, some of which are desirable in the long term too, some of which are not.

Leaders need to be able to define what 'it is working' looks like, and secure feedback mechanisms for the system so that everyone in the system can look at the evidence, and make adjustments/adapt collectively. If you only pay attention to money, money is what you organise around.

We propose that feedback mechanisms incorporate:

1. Indicators set for the system as a whole (these may be targets/star ratings)
2. Indicators of how well the system is working with identity/relationships/information.

Finally the leadership task is to **help the system understand the impact of its actions** ie have access to itself. Leaders can do this by taking time to review with others in the system using evidence-based conversations. Simply ask the questions:

1. 'What happened?' – map the intended and unintended consequences of decisions/strategies; undertake a full learning review.
2. 'What have we learnt about ourselves as a system?'.

"Process is the technology that allows the manipulation of our energies and wisdom." With deference to Malidoma Some.

References, reading, resources

Some, M.P. & Some, L.M. (1991) *The Healing Wisdom of Africa*. Jeremy Tarcher.
Wheatley, M. & Kellner-Rogers, M. (1996) *The Irresistable Future of Organizing*. July/August at http://www.margretwheatley.com/articles/irresistiblefuture.html.

Change in systems

- Change happens.
- It happens because the system's identity gets perturbed by something that resonates internally. It is contextual.
- All change is a change in identity.
- Resistance to change is, therefore, predictable, necessary and certain.
- Resistance to change is not negative.
- Change in dynamic systems cannot be managed (fixed, sorted, planned exactly).

Interestingly, since we spend so much time fixing symptoms, we can easily miss the really fundamental change waiting to happen, or actually happening around us.

What if we spent more time working out the question, the answer for which would make a real difference? So, let's think about it like this. Something is going on, and within the system, someone/people are asking for and identifying changes that need to happen. Let's say it's the fact that there is no commissioning strategy for older people in a health economy. Some members of the system think this is wrong and needs to be re-addressed. However every time they try to put together a group to develop a commissioning strategy, few turn up and those that do don't have the power to get any strategy implemented. The context they identify is that any new strategy will identify a huge gap between need and provision, which at the moment is buried in the system because older people don't count. So, what is the issue here? Is it that they don't have a strategy – well obviously this is wrong, but tackling it at this level just isn't working. The task here is to find the question that gets to the cause. Perhaps the question is: 'Why is it that older people don't count here?' This in itself is a punishing question. It implies people don't care and should be found out. It's probably much more complex than that, and is buried in historical relationships. In finding the question, members from the system have to sit down and work through the history and context, working out what question it is that will get to the cause and will invite people in to take part in answering it. For more about asking meaningful questions, see below.

Once the question is clear, you may find that the system that is relevant to that question is different than the one you first identified. In working out what the system is that needs to be engaged in answering the question, we identify all who have a real interest and who can make any change work together. You know that you own what you create. Identifying who the 'owners' are for the question leads you straight into a change process that works with all those who are part of the identity that has to change early on.

The next question is: 'Does the system know it's a system?'. Does everyone that you have identified know about each other; know the part they each play; know the implications of their actions on each other?

Then we get onto: 'Does the system have access to itself?' Can it change – does it know enough about itself to change? We talk about identity (does the membership act as though it belongs together, or is it a mismatch of warring factions!), relationships (are there mature relationships of respect; is there ability to work with different views and perspectives; where does power lie?), information (are there data available about how the system works now?).

Finally for any change effort the remaining question is: 'What wants to happen?'. Here we propose that the energy is in the system to change itself. If all the above work has been done, then new behaviours and patterns will emerge and be acted on.

The change process therefore comprises:

1. What is the question?
2. What is the relevant system (for that question)?
3. Does the system know it's a system?
4. Does it have access to itself?
   – information
   – relationships
   – self-reference (feedback and learning)
5. What wants to happen?

Wheatley & Rogers (1996/7)

A story

Jane Keep was commissioned to develop an OD strategy for a local government agency in London. The request for an external person to write an OD strategy allowed the 'agency' to abdicate responsibility for developing it and for using the journey of developing the OD strategy as part of the OD development for the organisation. Jane therefore spent time working out the 'real' question by exploring why the agency wanted an OD strategy. After a number of meetings and discussions 'brainstorming the questions', a new question was found: 'How can we develop organisational development capacity within our organisation … so that we can in future write our own OD strategies…?'. This was still felt not to be the key underlying question. Further exploratory meetings and discussions explored the second question to reveal a further underlying question: 'We are a bright intelligent organisation – we have many strategies and processes and excellent managers – but why do we not "get things done"?'. This then became the question.

Jane then 're-contracted' with the organisation to explore this issue with a number of potential future OD champions who could then develop a diagnostic/questioning approach so that they could develop their own OD strategy to meet the real underlying need of the organisation. Had Jane 'dived' straight into write the OD strategy the organisation would a) have continued in the same cycle adding to their policies, but not delivering; b) distracted themselves by developing OD capacity as yet another 'resource' but still have an organisation that didn't 'get things done' when by looking at the underlying issue they can start to fulfil more than one issue – but most of all 'get things done'. Time taken to 'brainstorm the question' built more capacity than taking questions on face value.

Jane Keep, Management Consultant

See also the section on 'Practice principles and insights' for tips on how to do this work.

Asking meaningful questions

In the mechanistic world, life revolves around having the right answer rather than having the right question. Actually how this is operationalised in organisations can be just having any answer! In systems work, we start by focusing on the powerful question that needs an answer (Brown, J. et al, 2005). In complex systems you find the answer by uncovering different ways of understanding what is really happening; by finding new ways of working; by thinking differently; by being creative. Often we are seeking answers or solutions to issues that are just symptoms of something deeper. Our quick fix answers lead us into more messy problems, as the knock-on effects in the system become apparent. By finding out what the question is that the system needs an answer for, we do several things:

1. We have to develop an understanding of the context.
2. We delve more deeply into the causalities.
3. We surface underlying assumptions
4. We open up the possibility for new thinking and ideas.

In addition, if we find the truly powerful question for the system, it generates energy in the system.

What makes a question powerful?

Firstly, the construction of the question moves from 'yes/no' questions to 'why', 'how', and 'what' questions. As an example consider the following sequence.

> Are you satisfied with our working relationship?
> When have you been most satisfied with your working relationship?
> What is it about our working relationship that you find most satisfying?
> Why might it be that our working relationship has had its ups and downs?

Vogt, Brown & Issacs (2003)

The second dimension is the scope – i.e. what system are we engaging here?

The third is the underlying assumptions that shape the question, that in essence lead into responses. Does the question challenge or confirm assumptions, and is that the intent of the question?

In designing a question we suggest that you focus on these issues. They come from work on the Public Conversations Project explained in *The Art of Powerful Questions*, by Vogt, Brown & Isaacs.

- Is this question relevant to the real life and real work of the people who will be exploring it?
- Is this a genuine question – a question to which I/we really don't know the answer?
- What 'work' do you want this question to do?
- Is this question likely to invite fresh thinking/feeling?
- What assumptions are embedded in the question?

References, resources, reading

Brown, J., with Isaacs, D. and the World Café Community (2005) *The World Café: Shaping Our Futures Through Conversations That Matter*. Berret-Koehler.

Vogt, E.E., Brown, J. & Isaacs, D.; illustrations by Nancy Margulies (2003) *The Art of Powerful Questions: Catalyzing Insight, Innovation, and Action*. Whole Systems Associates.

Pratt, J., Gordon, P. Plamping, D. (1999) *Working Whole Systems. Putting Theory into Practice in Organisations*. London: King's Fund Publishing.

Wheatley, M. & Kellner-Rogers, M. (1996/7) *Notes from the Self Organising Systems Seminars*. Utah: Sundance.

Designing interventions

Design and facilitation

The design of any change effort will call on a number of practices depending on the stage of the work. In the following section we offer a range of practices that you can use in the design of your change effort, though rarely do any of these stand alone. You may design workshops that use several of the practices. You may design a change process that incorporates multiple practices in its various stages. In addition we offer tips to facilitating these practices in the section following on practice principles and insights.

The design of any change effort requires working through the stages of change we identified above, designing the conversations at each stage iteratively.

1. What is the question?
2. What is the relevant system (for that question)?
3. Does the system know it's a system?
4. Does it have access to itself?
   - information
   - relationships
   - self-reference (feedback and learning)
5. What wants to happen?

Wheatley & Kellner-Rogers (1996/7)

Design principles

The first, and perhaps most controversial, principle of planning in this work is that the individual both makes the collective, and is made by the collective. In essence, individuals do not exist apart from and outside the social. The starting point for all the design work here is the social – i.e. the system, not the individual. Understanding the individual's behaviour separate from the system they are operating in is just not possible. All of the design starts with the system. Whilst there will be moments for individuals to quietly reflect on their actions, this is always in the context of this system here and now.

The next principle for design is that change requires robust effective relationships. This is the bit that takes the longest. In designing change efforts, what you are trying to do all the way through is to design conversations and actions that generate these relationships in the system.

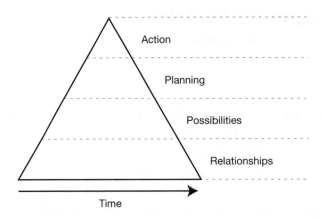

Source: Adapted from Knowledge Based Development Co. Ltd

Relationship triangle

Taking time thinking through the sorts of relationships you need for this work, and designing interventions that will lead you to those relationships is critical for this work to be effective. The design for any change effort reflects what you think matters in change– who, what, how – in effecting the change. So paying attention at the outset to the design and how it matches your own beliefs about change, and how it models the desired behaviours is critical. For instance if you truly believe that you need everyone who has an idea to voice it, then you have to create a process where people feel confident enough to share their idea; where everyone will get truly listened to; where hierarchy doesn't matter. The design of the process gets you the results you deserve.

This is the most time-consuming part of any change effort. Design, reflection, checking out, redesign. All this adds up to much quicker and meaningful action. If you design well, you will surface all the possibilities; enable the system to truly access itself to find the best answer and to take action that will work. This means that you cannot design alone. You need a small team of people prepared to work together on the design so that you can do the following.

There are a number of key areas that you need to consider when designing change interventions:

1. Surface the patterns of behaviour that are evident in the system – find ways of making the system's current behaviour apparent to all systems' players, and work on what is causing these patterns. If you don't name them, and work out which ones are helpful and which ones are getting in the way, they will keep popping up in the new work.

2. Don't get wedded to the first question that you uncover. In working with a system to find out the meaningful question, you will find that the first one you work on leads you to new questions that also need attention. Design the work so that you can pay attention to questions as they arise, and that can adapt questions as you begin to explore them.

3. Make sure you take time to create feedback loops – i.e. is the work and design playing out in the way you expected/wanted/congruent with the change you desired? How will you know?

If you are designing for the whole system, then there are a number of key areas you need to consider. Firstly and most importantly, if it's a whole systems approach, you need to address the whole system. People come and participate as active participants in the system not as representatives. The people come because the work is meaningful to them. You invite participants to reflect the makeup of the system for the issue you are working on. For the process to work you are seeking active participation and dialogue in relation to the participants' role as a part (i.e. delivering their bit of the system) **and** as a whole (their responsibility for the functioning of the system as a whole). The only work of a whole system approach is the real time work that needs to be done now. Whole systems approaches are not 'about' work; they are doing the work in the room linked by the system's explicit core purpose and implicit principles of organising. Finally a whole systems approach is one of co-production – the participants together produce the results; it does not get referred to another body to take decisions and action. All whole systems approaches lead to action that is co-produced (from Diane Plamping, *Not Working Whole Systems*).

Finally, in this work we suggest you ensure personal supervision either one-to-one, or through a peer network of others doing this sort of work. Undoubtedly, as with all systems work, as you get into it, you become systems blind, i.e. multiple options for design get narrowed by the system you become part of. Supervision helps you keep the multiple options open, and helps you design work that is safe.

Set up

For each of the following practices we have talked about the room layout. When doing any work with groups, at minimum you need to design the space as well as the process. You will need a space that:

- has plenty of natural light;
- has plenty of water available, and regular tea/coffee (free flowing is best) with snacks – if the session includes lunch then make sure this is in a different room;
- has plenty of wall space for you to stick both flip charts and larger pieces of paper – at minimum 10ft × 6ft wall spaces;
- has materials for writing on charts – you need plenty of pens, and you will need to bring masking tape for putting charts up on the wall;
- has disabled access;
- has room temperature control; and
- can provide round tables that are no more than 5ft diameter (we work with 4ft or nothing). Don't ever compromise on the 6ft wedding tables – they just don't work for conversations – you can barely see each other across them, let alone hear each other. Also don't go for rectangle tables – it recreates hierarchy.

Make sure the size of space is right for the group – you need a level of intimacy that ensures conversations take place, but not so cosy that it's claustrophobic, nor so large that you feel a very small and insignificant group!

Facilitation

In facilitating the practices in this toolkit, the facilitator's role is to:

- Let the system access itself.
- Keep time boundaries (keep focused on the task).
- Ensure that the questions are clear and unambiguous, and invite conversation.
- Let the process run – don't get drawn into expert roles, or manage out difficult/diverse views, or step into silence inappropriately.
- Hold for depth – if the conversation keeps moving back to symptoms, keep your focus on causalities, and guide the conversation back.
- Manage anxiety appropriately. You will need and want some anxiety, but you don't want it at the level that people disengage. Neither do you want anger, because what you are doing is not what was expected. Focus on clar-

ifying expectations, being explicit about purpose, and giving clear direction (just like the leadership role). Make the work of the conversation and the 'rules' by which you want people to converse explicit, simple and available.

- Model behaviour at all times. Take to your feet and walk about.

The next section on Practice Principles describes how to design with these principles in mind. But before that there is one more aid to facilitation that we believe to be really useful in helping the system see itself – Strategic illustration.

References and resources

Plamping, D. *Not Working Whole Systems*. Urban Partnerships Group. Unpublished.

Strategic illustration

Strategic illustration uses text and images as powerful tools to help organisations or individuals deal with complexity, aid intellectual growth, and deliver innovative and timely results. It is a unique, new process that facilitates the natural ways people perceive, learn, create new concepts, listen, and collaborate.

Who benefits?

Anyone who wants to heighten the effectiveness of their organisation. In particular, strategic illustration has been successfully employed by small businesses, corporations, dot-coms, nonprofits, community and religious organisations, government organisations, individuals and more. It is especially useful in augmenting the results of team building, conflict resolution, visioning, strategic planning, problem-solving, analysis, decision making, redesign, idea generating, consensus-building, looking at timelines and forecasting future trends.

How does it work?

A strategic illustrator works in conjunction with a facilitator or consultant to give the meeting, presentation, or event direction and form. During a meeting, as it unfolds, the illustrator creates highly visual recordings, shaping the information into a map of the thought process. He/she captures key ideas in vibrant images and words on mural-sized pieces of wall-hung paper, using felt-tipped markers and other media. Participants are then able to scan a real-time, ongoing record of the meeting as it develops. This immediately changes the nature and quality of the meeting: a group's potential is optimised as everyone literally works on the 'same page' to create a collective vision. When all members are involved and interested, the group as a whole is enriched, and therefore better able to find creative, new solutions to existing problems.

The process of strategic illustration does not end there. After the meeting, the murals can be made available to stakeholders, in the form of a page-sized photograph, a report, or a computer file. This record serves as a valuable memory tool and a useful, easy-to-understand document to be shared with others.

Strategic illustration brings about results in several crucial ways:

- **It presents a clear image.** Visual language, understood with minimal time and effort, is unrivalled in its efficiency to capture an idea's essence. Through the application of colour, shape, visual metaphors, spatial relationships, icons, diagramming and other tools of visual language *as well as* the use of text, strategic illustration distils and organises complex issues. By drawing out patterns and relationships, it synthesises information, taking issues from the abstract and individual to the concrete, actionable, and collective. A group gets instant, ongoing feedback so that they can conceptualise more quickly, synthesise larger amounts of data and insure faster movement of analysis. In addition, visual language communicates quickly and effectively across disciplines and cultures, uniting and focusing diverse individuals.

- **It helps to create a shared vision.** Strategic illustration stimulates 'big picture thinking'. The neutral role of the illustrator – their willingness to include all participants' ideas on an equal basis – creates trust and stimulates participation. As a 'public' record – a flexible framework capable of storing and displaying diverse ideas – strategic illustration pulls together many perspectives while at the same time aligning group members. Participants can see details in their context – see, so to speak, the forest *and* the trees simultaneously, and through doing so, reconcile opposing ideas, achieve consensus and develop a common understanding. Strategic illustration creates a team that is fully engaged, aligned, and grounded.

- **It engages creative thinking.** In the same way that the notation style used in 'mind mapping' releases individual creativity, the wall charts created in strategic illustration enhance group and team creativity. Metaphors and imagery stimulate the right side of the brain and excite intuitive, spontaneous, and imaginative thinking. Strategic illustration, utilising both words and images, energises the full application of cortical skills and encourages a fusion of creative and analytical thinking. As a result, communication happens on a deeper level. This stimulates participants to 'think outside the box', to enact change on a committed, emotional level, and to come up with innovative solutions which lead to real results. Strategic illustration transforms value into action.

- **It enhances memory**, on both an individual and group level, and creates a record to remember by and share. It is said that people can easily hold two to five ideas at once in the mind, but up to fifteen on paper. In addition, strategic illustration, both beautiful and orderly, stimulates attention and focus in a group. By consolidating information into aesthetically pleasing, 'mind sized' pieces, and showing relationships between those pieces, strategic illustration allows participants to absorb more information during a meeting, information that will then be remembered better later. It is especially useful for individuals with a 'visual' memory. Strategic illustration also provides continuity in a meeting, so that members can pick up where they left off at breaks, and latecomers can catch up.

"Now that the meeting is over, what do I do with these charts?"

Another important aspect of the strategic illustration process is the documentation made available to stakeholders after a meeting is over: as a page-sized image, a report, or a computer file. The murals that were generated in the meeting become the source or reference point for ongoing conversations and group decision-making after a meeting. This enables stakeholders to build on what was said before without having to start from scratch each time. This documentation can also be shared with others who were not in the meeting to link them to the thinking behind the work to which they are contributing.

Practice principles and insights

In 1996, people working across the world on large-scale systems change came together to share their learning and experiences. A number of the principles and insights discussed there resonate with our own experience. These principles and insights underpin all of the practices described in this book. We find that they act as a useful checklist as we design new work, or adapt the practices described here, and we suggest that you use them in the same way.

1. Hold the intention.
2. Focus on the real work.
3. Use meaningful measures.
4. Create a spirit of inquiry and learning.
5. Appreciate what works.
6. Develop common language, images, metaphors.
7. Encourage ongoing reflection and conversation.

From *Strategic Dialogue on Large-Scale Systems Change* (1996)

Hold the intention

Keep coming back to the purpose of the work. Be clear about the question you are working on. Check back that the processes you are engaged on help you answer the big question at the core of your work. Develop principles out of your values and purpose that act as a guide to action. Seek congruency in your actions. Wait for the answers to emerge; be patient.

Focus on the real work

Start with what's happening now. Pay attention to people's daily work and concerns. Deeply understand the now, looking for evidence from multiple places. Don't get caught up all the time in what might be, use this only as a context for what is.

Utilise meaningful measures

Find and develop qualitative and quantitative measures that help you understand what is happening and the impact of your processes. Look for stories and facts. Generate shared ownership of the measures. Inquire together on the interpretation of the evidence. Have evidence-based conversations (what do we really know about what is going on here). Make space for surprises; don't exclude information that pops up. Review the measures to see if they are offering all that you need. Use the measures as a way of understanding, not of punishing or rewarding. Make the measures available to all.

Create a spirit of inquiry and learning

Make the most of people's natural curiosity and desire for things to work. Craft powerful questions rather than provide the right answers. Continually clarify and explore underlying assumptions and beliefs. What do we know here and now about how change happens around here? Find ways of sharing learning; make space for reflection as legitimate work.

Create conditions for healthy feedback. Embed reflection in all business processes. Balance urgency and reflection.

Appreciate what works

Focus on what's possible; what's trying to happen here. Find the places where there is energy for change. Make the most of what's working. Share stories of successes; find out what helped that happen. Look for small changes and link and connect these together.

Develop common language, core images, and metaphors

Find ways of describing and analysing what's happening with those involved. Create language around the issue that is meaningful to all taking part. Look for simple, clear ideas and images that capture complex issues. Look for images and metaphors that attract attention and draw into the future.

Encourage ongoing conversation

Talking is doing. Developing the relationships is the business. Design processes for conversation that are fit for the work to be done. Energise conversations through process. Ground conversations in lived experiences. Make the most of people's ability to work in dialogue. Focus on listening intently and respectfully.

Reference

Strategic Dialogue on Large-Scale Systems Change. 1996. Unpublished report of a working group.

Practices

Practice	Purpose	Size of group
Some core practices for groups and teams		
Dialogue	Create collective understanding	Any size
Guiding principles for personal feedback	To make sense of personal impact. To improve group impact.	One to one, small work groups
Evidence-based conversations	To generate a truly shared picture of reality. To uncover the operating principles.	For teams/task groups
Organisational feedback	To get more of what you pay attention to	Leadership group
Conversations for understanding and learning		
Intended/unintended consequences	As feedback mechanism to inform principles and decisions.	For teams/task groups
Communities of practice	For a system to deepen its knowledge and expertise by interacting on an ongoing basis.	To reflect the size of the system.
Mapping/pattern spotting	Help see the place each plays in the system, and the system's inherent complexity	To reflect the system to be explored.
Co-consulting groups	Explore personal impact. Understand causalities.	Groups of 6–7 members.
Organisational visits	To help understand your own organisation better.	Groups of 6–8 members
Conversations for possibility		
Café	Conversations to surface possibility	Minimum 15 to >100
Future search	Form the common ground for players in a system to work together.	Large group
Conversational conferences	Maximise the potential of networks, and the possibility of expertise in a system	Medium and large groups

(continued)

Practice	Purpose	Size of group
Conversations to determine values/principles/agreements		
Gathering stories	Uncovering lived values in a system, system's identity.	In groups of 6 × 1; >10
Inquiring into promising practices	Organised inquiry into making most of what is promising in a system.	Teams of 2 in groups of 6 × 1; >10
Identifying guiding principles	Identify system principles and agreements to govern decisions and practices	Large group currently working in the system
Conversations for action		
Open space	Process for a system to work on key complex question where there are diverse views	20 to >100
Real time strategic change	Strategy development – designing sustainable change.	As many from the system as possible
Appreciative interviewing	To amplify what works in a system.	Groups of 3 × 1; >30
Positive difference and problem solving	To move a system with a contentious issue from aggressive opposition to active problem solving.	Medium and large groups
Positive deviance	Finding out what works in a system and doing more of it	Small to large groups

Some core practices for groups and teams

Dialogue

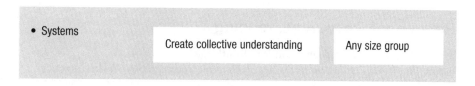

- Systems
  Create collective understanding | Any size group

One of the most simple practices is that of dialogue which is at the beginning of a meeting sitting in a circle and as an American friend of ours calls it 'checking in'. It brings all those in the meeting together, taking note of what's going on in everyone's lives, the context to being in the room. Noting together what resonates for each other, telling stories about work or things going on outside work, reflecting on what has been said and heard. In essence taking time to understand each other and the context in which the group works together.

> Dialogue is a conversation with a centre, not sides.
>
> Isaacs

So dialogue is a process of creating collective understanding. It has at its heart a number of basic rules (these are based on the MIT Dialogue Project's Guidelines for Dialogue):

1. Listen in order to understand. Don't listen just to jump in with your point – waiting for the gap in the conversation; listen in order to fully understand where each and every one is coming from. Listen deeply when you disagree.
2. Listen to the whole – what patterns are emerging?
3. Listen for and seek connections between the threads, ideas, parts.
4. Listen to your own listening – what do you filter out? What grates/creates anxiety? What excites?
5. Suspend assumptions and judgements – Do you only note what confirms your assumptions? Are you open to having those assumptions questioned?
6. Slow down the inquiry; take time to hear everyone and to make sense of what is being said. Take time to reflect and to think about what you say.
7. Make sense collectively – look together for what is behind what is being said. Ask questions that help illuminate what is happening.

Dialogue is useful when trying to deal with a difficult problem, when you need to be secure in your actions, when things aren't working out the way you thought they were going to, when relationships in a group are getting in the way of the work.

References, resources, reading

Bohm, D. (2000) *On Dialogue.* London: Routledge.

Isaacs, W. (1999) *Dialogue and the Art of Thinking Together.* New York: Currency and Doubleday.

Guiding principles and rules for personal feedback

• Cognition • Autopoiesis	To make sense of personal impact. To improve group impact.	One to one; small work groups.

Why feedback?

Feedback is a powerful process for making sense of the impact of your behaviours. It helps clarify your own identity and can be used to uncover your own beliefs about change in systems. It is also one of the most effective ways of inviting others to change their behaviour towards you.

Feedback itself is an intervention in a relationship. It is equally appropriate to seek feedback about your own behaviour as it is to offer feedback to someone as to the impact of their behaviour on you.

There is no single hidden truth you are uncovering in this process. The inquirer and their colleagues giving feedback both hold their own reality about the events that are being recalled as evidence. They see events through the lens of their own identity. The inquirer may have meant a behaviour to have a particular impact. The colleague may well have a different perception about the impact, based on for instance previous experiences, personal judgements about what matters or own theories of change.

> In a meeting someone had made a joke, the purpose of which (in their eyes) was to relieve an impossibly tense situation, so that the meeting could regroup and move on. A colleague giving feedback felt that the meeting was just getting to the difficult stuff that needed surfacing in order to reach clarity and a decision. She felt the 'joke' was a way of pulling out of having the difficult conversation that needed to take place.

Feedback says as much about the person giving feedback as the person it is given to. It is therefore helpful to see feedback as a conversation to uncover as far as possible the felt impact of behaviour in order for the inquirer to decide if they want to change that behaviour (or not!).

Whilst we are all reasonably fluent and eloquent, feedback is a very designed and focussed intervention, not to be confused with praise, or criticism, which themselves can be legitimate and appropriate at points in a relationship, but which are not feedback.

Some core rules of feedback

1. All feedback has to contain an 'YOU – I' bit, (e.g. When you...I felt).
2. Feedback is only offered on observable behaviours – unambiguous descriptions of actions taken or words said. It often starts with the form "When **you** did/said..."). It is critical to leave out interpretations. So for instance you would say: "When you slammed your fist on the table......", not: "When you were angry" as this latter statement is your interpretation of what was behind the action; it is your own assumption.
3. This description is completed by a statement about the impact on you. Continuing our example: "When you slammed your fist on the table it made **me** feel........(anxious ...angry...patronised....supported)"
4. Feedback is about both those behaviours that had a positive impact on you as well as those that did not. So for instance it may be that you say: "When you smiled at me in that meeting, I felt that you supported what I was saying."
5. What follows is a conversation where you can both explore what happened and your assumptions, interpretations.
6. It may be helpful (but is not necessary) to say what change you would find helpful.

So when you give someone feedback it is important not to use evaluations (you were so good at chairing the meeting), generalisations (you always/never...) or abstractions (you are so clever/stupid/...) but to use **concrete describable behaviours** (when you interrupted/didn't tell me the test result that afternoon). Equally you need the courage to be truthful as to the **emotional impact** of their behaviour on you.

Choosing to give feedback

It is worth keeping the following in mind when considering whether to give feedback:

- Is the focus of the feedback behaviour that can be changed? (e.g. it might be reasonable to feed back to someone that you have difficulty following

them when they speak quickly, it is not appropriate to offer feedback about their accent).
- It is helpful to give feedback about behaviours that you want more of – behaviour that can be amplified because of its positive impact.
- Observe the impact the feedback is having and make personal judgements as to how much feedback to offer (one or two behaviours is usually more than enough at any time).

Differences between feedback and criticism

Feedback is:
- Specific
- Descriptive
- Clear

Criticism is:
- General
- Judgmental
- Personal
- Blaming

Feedback often requires repeated conversations. If one party chooses to change any behaviour, they will need to make sense of the impact of that change too.

Evidence-based conversations – learning review

With thanks to Myron Rogers

| • Autopoieisis
• Cognition
• Social
• Dissipative | To generate a truly shared picture of reality.
To uncover the operating principles. | For teams/task groups. |

A learning review has its roots in the US Army's 'After Action Review'. It is an evidence-based conversation that examines a significant action a team/group has taken to generate a shared picture of reality. From this shared view, we then collectively explore the assumptions, relationships, identity and information rules that generate the consequences – intended or otherwise – of the action. This work typically results in an answer to the question: "Who are we *really*?" that both surprises and allows for new choices and strategies for change. It reveals the *operating* agreements about how to be together in the work and what work matters. These operating agreements are seldom what we consciously choose.

We interpret events from our own set of assumptions. Without getting clear together about who we are in our work together, and how we are actually working together, choices for working differently are ineffective, since we haven't exposed the collective dynamics that produce any outcomes. We just drag the current dynamics into the future work, and enter a new cycle of unintended consequences. An effective learning review can get at the source of unintended consequences, and enable new and effective choices for creating the conditions that will deliver the future we intend for each other and our organisation. In addition the learning review is focused forward, generating lessons that can be used immediately by the group/team.

A learning review has a number of key characteristics:

*   It is not about blame and judgement. The purpose is to discover why what happened, happened.
*   It focuses on a recent/current task.
*   It allows all who took part to contribute and learn.

We recommend that learning reviews become part of the work pattern of teams and groups.

The process

The process is simple. It answers four questions, and creates the conditions for a new path of action.

1. *What was supposed to happen?*
   This first task clarifies the shared understanding of what was expected. Using project plans, specifications, shared briefs, you begin using the evidence as a source of understanding.

2. *What really happened?*
   The first task is to construct a shared picture of what really happened. This is not an interpretative or evaluative exercise. It rests on the assumption that everyone involved has critical *but only partial* information and experience. Until we construct a whole picture of what happened from many viewpoints, we have no basis for collective learning and change. Individual learning from a particular event does not constitute organisational learning – it tends only to fragment, as each of us learns something unique from our view of events. When we have a shared picture of the details of what happened, we can begin to understand the power of collective action to support or thwart our best intentions.

   This involves writing down collectively step by step what actually happened sequentially, without going into why it happened like that, or what could have been different. The discipline here is to just write up what happened when (including specific actions/emails/conversations).

3. *Why did it happen this way?*
   Working from this shared event map, we can explore many dynamics that led to the outcomes. We can inquire deeply into what the agreements about how to be in the work together are (relationship rules). We can map the information flows and determine the information rules. We can see what we really value, based on the work we are doing, not on our aspirations. From this, the choices of what and how to change, what new agreements we need and how to use them, become clearer.

4. *What have we learned (and what do we change)?*
   We enter into a conversation about key learnings, and what and how to change the system to generate outcomes that more clearly serve our intent. There is generally good learning about systems dynamics here – how individual intent and action is usually not responsible for outcomes, but how

our combined actions add up to outcomes no one intended. We see organisational problems not as individual ineffectiveness, but collective unconsciousness. As a strategy for change, we look at what to keep that serves us, what to change to serve us better, and what to abandon. A new set of agreements and tactics for how to work together can emerge.

Resources

Parry, C., Darling, M. (2001) Emergent learning in action: the after action review, *The Systems Thinker*, **12**, 8, October, pp. 1–5.

A Leader's Guide To After Action Review (TC 25-20) (1993) Department of the Army.

http://www.nelh.nhs.uk/knowledge_management/km2/aar_toolkit.asp

Organisational feedback

• Autopoeisis • Cognition	To get more of what you pay attention to	Leadership group

Organisational feedback is a powerful practice in determining organisational behaviour. As we know that where organisations set targets and measure them, the organisation as a whole organises to deliver these targets. In essence you get more of whatever it is you pay attention to. If it's not measured, it doesn't matter. Whilst that sounds very crude, in effect if you look at your organisation's executive team and board meetings, you get a real sense of what matters to that organisation – what counts literally.

This exercise is to review what actually counts in your organisation – and if that doesn't align with your organisation's key purpose and values, to reshape the organisation's feedback processes.

1. Firstly, as the top team, individually write down what you think the organisation exists to do, and what you think you pay attention to corporately.
2. Gather together the visible evidence of where you collectively and individually focus your attention and efforts. For instance take the last six months Board meeting agendas; the last six months' executive team meeting agendas; your own diaries over the last month; every corporate communication that you have sent out.
3. Analyse these and work out where you are expending the most effort (what issues); some effort; little effort (i.e. it doesn't feature much in your analysis). In analysing your diaries, we suggest that you actually add up the time spent on each issue over the month.
4. Put these up on the wall mapping them out from lots of effort/attention to little effort/attention. What are the patterns/surprises? What does it say about your work effort? At this stage don't get defensive about what you see. This is not to see how you match up to your purpose in order to feel bad. The process is designed to recognise that top teams can drift and be caught up by issues of the moment, without thinking about how it all adds up together.

5. What's missing? How does the focus compare to your first statements about what you think your corporate work is about?

We often find that a missing part is learning. Organisations say that they value learning and want learning to be a core part of their organisational culture. However, when you look at the feedback loops currently in place – what the top team pays attention to, you may struggle to find topics that relate to learning on the agenda. If the organisation was really interested in learning you might see topics such as:

- New initiatives
- What we can celebrate this month
- Paper describing the learning from a big corporate development (e.g. PFI) and how that will apply to other areas.
- Initiatives to share learning e.g. communities of practice.
- Development opportunities taken by staff this month.
- Shadowing experiences undertaken, and actions arising from these.

Mostly public sector organisations are dominated by budgets, with less attention being paid to health outcomes.

So, if as an organisation you have a view about how you want the organisation to do its business, then where you pay attention – what feedback loops you create for the top team – is critical to that organisation's behaviour. Systems notice only what is important to them, so start thinking what your own analysis is saying about what you think counts, and how you want to change that.

There are a number of principles to creating organisational feedback:

1. It must relate congruently and coherently to the organisation's purpose and values.
2. The feedback areas and process needs to be reviewed constantly – it is contextual, it needs to change over time.
3. It can become rigid, meaning that the organisation doesn't capture feedback that allows it to adapt. You need to design feedback that enables surprises and new information to get in.
4. Making sense of data acquired in the feedback process requires the whole organisation to take part. The top team can make sense to a point, but engaging the whole organisation enables you to choose action collectively; to develop the feedback process; to change behaviour i.e. to organise around the feedback quickly.

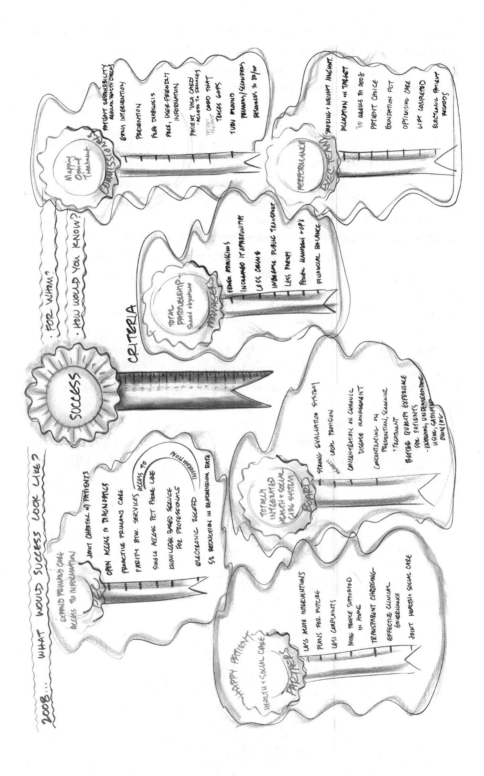

The first step is to work out together what 'success' would look like for your organisation. Describing it richly, so that it can be shared widely.

The next step is to work out the categories that matter to you that will help you know if you are getting there. Work out where you need feedback data. One PCT's example of the areas they designed feedback for is:

1. Performance management – the targets, and the required performance.
2. Effective services – how effective are our services?
3. Contracting – are we getting what we should be getting out of this process?
4. Workforce – are our staff engaged, feeling part of the organisation, making the most of their capacity and potential?
5. Corporate citizenship – how are we working together as a whole?
6. Effective partnerships – how effective are we in our partnerships?
7. Learning, creativity and innovation – are we making the most of the ideas in the organisation?
8. Fit for the future – how well are we doing preparing ourselves for the future?
9. Information – are we organising information to support our work?

For each of these they again defined what 'success' would look like, and how they would know if they were successful, working out what information they needed, in what format and how often.

This process in effect informs the governance of the organisation. What matters here, how will we know how we are doing, what does this tell us about where we need to focus our efforts.

Conversations for
understanding and learning

Intended/unintended consequences

• Systems • Autopoiesis	As feedback mechanism to inform principles and decisions.	For teams/task groups

Systems rely on feedback to know how to act. All too often we get caught up in taking decisions and in acting, without looking at the impact of that decision/act. Moreover when we do look for feedback, or to monitor action, we look for the intended actions/impact, without looking for what else happened as well.

Simply, this process asks task groups to take a particular decision/action/ strategy and ask these questions:

- Did it have the expected impact (the intended consequences)?
- What other things happened that were definitely and probably another result of this (unintended consequences)?

When both the intended and unintended consequences have been mapped out, the task group can ask itself how much of the unintended were positive to the process. For the ones that were not, or that caused other problems, what could the group have done to factor them out at the start? In addition does the group want to change any of its principles that govern its decisions? What has the group learnt about how this system works. Finally what implications does this have for future decisions/action – for instance what context information does the group need in the future?

Communities of practice

With thanks to Etienne Wenger

- Systems
- Autopoeises

For a system to deepen its knowledge and expertise by interacting on an ongoing basis

Size of group to reflect the system.

Communities of practice are groups of people working in a system together who share a passion about a concern, topic, issue who deepen their knowledge and expertise by interacting (discussing, sharing information, helping each other) on an ongoing basis. The basis for the design of communities of practice is that learning is a social act, it requires us to engage together in real time with others to find out individually and collectively how to put into practice ideas/approaches/knowledge. In effect change requires a conversation across all players to understand what's happening and how it's happening. Organisation have a role in connecting communities of practice together, and learning about the impact of their work on the organisation as a whole. Membership of a community of practice implies commitment to the domain of that community.

Practice in this context means creating meaning (why we do this work together), creating coherence (how we do our work together), and for learning (what works and why – and how do new members learn about our work). Community means a group working in real time on real work in the same location, but also at another scale – groups working on the same work in different locations, learning together. In essence the groups take responsibility for the knowledge they need to do their work.

The basic principles for communities of practice are:

1. Participation – everyone in the community has a voice, can be heard and can contribute to the practice. Difference explored.
2. Commitment to practice – to uncovering what the work it, why we do it, how it's done, and to reciprocity with others wanting to learn.
3. Understanding boundaries and scale – what works here and does it change as the scale changes for instance if the boundary to the community changes.

4. Reflection using evidence-based conversations as a core practice in itself.
5. Creativity as a source of energy for practice – using imagination, permission to explore, finding new ways of exploring work.

So communities of practice are networks of members committed to learning how to do the best they can in their domain of interest creating relationships for learning and development, and clarifying what information needs to be generated and shared across the community.

References, reading, resources

Wenger, E & Lave, M. (2002) *Communities of Practice. Learning, Meaning and Identity*. Cambridge: Cambridge University Press.
Background: http://www.ewenger.com/theory/index.htm
Communities of Practice: Learning as a social system
    http://www.co-i-l.com/coil/knowledge-garden/cop/lss.shtml

Mapping/pattern spotting

- Systems

| Help see the place each plays in the system, and the system's inherent complexity | Small to large groups, to reflect the system to be explored. |

There are several possible starting points to system mapping; each of them involves a real/near real scenario, depending on the question the system is working on. For instance:

- A scenario where a user/consumer first interfaces with the system being explored. Here you start with that moment in time, and ask: 'What happened next' with everyone mapping out their possible involvement over time. For instance a young person comes to a doctor's surgery with evidence of bruising.
- A decision that needs to be made, or has been made. For instance a partnership agreement; a decision to close a service; a decision to change a service.
- The amount of times partners meet and over what, in answer to a question focusing on how well they work together.

The practice requires all participants to work out what role they play, where they fit, and to begin to see the impact of what they do. Participants describe how the scenario might develop, or how it is playing out now, using a large wall chart with time notated on it.

For each intervention, action, the participants try to capture how that relates to others on the map (so connecting lines can be drawn to depict relationships for ideas, action, support, legal issues etc). The group chooses what dimensions they want to pay attention to. You can even draw several maps for the same issue to show different things/relationships. The point here is to describe what really happens in the system, not what is supposed to happen.

From mapping the next stage is to work on two key areas:

1. Patterns – what patterns are evident across the map (e.g. these could be patterns of ways of working – i.e. what takes precedence; or of relationships)
2. What questions does this map seek from us?

The purpose is to gain new insights into how the system currently works, in order to work through assumptions about what interventions individually or collectively would make a difference.

References, reading and resources

Pratt, J., Gordon, P., Plamping, D. (1999) *Working Whole Systems. Putting Theory into Practice in Organisations*. King's Fund Publishing.

Co-consulting groups

With thanks to David Knowles

• Cognition • Systems	Explore personal impact. Understand causalities.	Groups of 6–7 members.

Co-consulting is a designed reflection and learning process that enables you in groups with peers as partners to:

(a) Deepen your understanding of the impact of own behaviour.
(b) Improve your ability to see the multiplicity of causal factors at play in complex work issues.
(c) Enhance your skills in consulting to others.

Co-consulting groups use this designed process to work in turn on each group member's work issues, meeting at regular intervals to enable members to take action and bring the impact of that action into the reflection process. The process involves saying, questioning, thinking, doing, reflecting. The questioning is challenging and supportive. The premise is that the individual will learn better by uncovering their own ideas about how to act; their own patterns of behaviour; their own way of seeing how organisations work.

The process

Each member of the consulting group in turn has the attention of the group on their chosen issue. Each member also acts as consultant to the other members: observing, giving feedback, asking questions and opening up different ways of understanding the issue.

The group agrees at the outset of the session how the time is to be used. Each member will need at least 45 minutes for their own issue, and over the course of the co-consulting group's sessions, every member should have had a chance to work on their own issue.

The member presenting (client)

Firstly, pick an issue that would benefit from time in this process. Pick something that is proving complex to work on; that is not turning out how you expected; that is bothering you more than you would expect; that is new to you; where relationships are proving difficult; where you don't know the answer; where you are not fixed in your view about what to do.

When you have picked your issue, explain it as clearly as you can to the group, remembering to include:

- Your assumptions about what would happen at the outset.
- What actually is happening, and what you have done.
- Your interpretation of why key people are acting the way they are.
- What you feel about what's going on.
- What you have thought of doing, and why.

The consultants

Your role as a consultant to your colleague (client) is to help them to reach a deeper understanding of the issue and their choices of action. Your role is not to advise (as in many normal work situations) but to help the client reach their own conclusions. Whilst inevitably you will learn yourself in listening to your client, the focus for you is their learning, and so the questions you ask should remain focused on consulting to them!

The best way to keep this focus is to listen attentively to your client. Let the client, whose time it is, talk uninterrupted for as long as they need. Let your client tell you when they have finished talking. If your client is talking thoughtfully, or struggling to express something, or thinking, it may not be helpful to interrupt. He or she may need some silent time in the session to digest new thoughts.

When it's useful to intervene, ask questions that help them think and see the issue more deeply.

Use the 'who', 'what', 'when', 'how' questions. Ask them to evidence their views. For example:

'How do you know that?'
'Why do you think that?'
'Who else is involved?'
'What else could you do/have you thought of?'
'What would he/she say, if they were here?'
'What is the most important thing?'

'What would it look like if it was going better?'
'What would you really like to do?'
'Have you been in this sort of situation before?'
'What did you do then?'

A common temptation is to give advice and make suggestions. You may find that you feel certain that you know how to solve the client's problem. Do not give advice or what might be seen as orders or judgements. Avoid saying things like:

'You ought to….'
'I would …'
'It is obvious that….'
'You should not have….'

At the end of each consulting session reflect on the process, how well you thought you took up the role, and what you noticed about it.

The structure

Each presentation and consulting session takes at least 45 minutes. The structure is as follows:

1. The client presents their issue for up to 15 minutes without interruption from other members of the group.
2. The consultants have the opportunity for 5 minutes to ask the client questions of clarification, to make sure they have enough information about the issue.
3. The consultants move on to asking questions to enable the client to deepen their understanding of the underlying patterns of behaviour and actions. 30 minutes.
4. The client has 5 minutes to reflect on what they have been asked and what has come up for them. They then present to the rest of the group their thoughts and any planned actions. There should be the opportunity to come back to the impact of these at the next meeting of the group.

Associated reading

Revans, R. (1982) *Origins and Growth of Action Learning*, Sweden: Bratt-Institute fur Neues Lernen.

Organisational visits

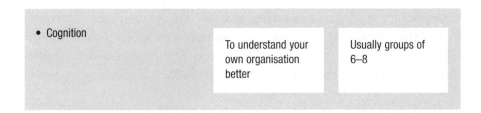

| • Cognition | To understand your own organisation better | Usually groups of 6–8 |

An organisational visit is a structured learning visit to another organisation by a leadership group. The purpose is to develop the group's insights and frameworks for understanding how organisations' work, in particular the identity of the organisation you are visiting; and your own leadership of wider organisational change.

The exercise also gives you an opportunity as a group to understand and learn from each other's ways of understanding and interpreting; and to learn from the process of working collaboratively as peers on a task.

In undertaking a visit, you may agree to offer the host organisation feedback as part of the process. In setting up the visit you will need to liase with someone in the host organisation that can set up the interviews and help you with logistics.

Briefing for the group undertaking the visit

Purpose

The visit will help you gain insights into how your own organisation works, by examining the challenges and opportunities that exist in the organisation you visit. As Proust wrote: "The real voyage of discovery lies not in seeking new landscapes, but in having new eyes", and this theme of expanding the way you make assumptions about organisations and leadership, is a consistent one for leaders. Often, seeing how another organisation operates gives you new insights and frameworks for understanding your own organisation and your own leadership.

The exercise also gives the visiting group an opportunity to understand and learn from each other's ways of understanding and interpreting,

The task

The task is for you to work as a whole group to come to conclusions about how the organisation you are visiting works, and how it works as part of a wider system (in health this could be the health economy). You visit the organisation as a whole, undertaking separate interviews in pairs. You have to make sense of how that organisation works, with a particular focus on how it works with others in its environment. You therefore need to undertake your interviews to make sense of that organisation for yourselves, as a whole group.

In essence each group interviews a cross-section of people from the organisation, and uses the information generated to make sense of how the organisation operates.

There are five stages:

1. Preparation
2. Interviews
3. Making sense
4. Presentations (to explore what you have learnt and how to make the most of it).
5. Process review.

1. Preparation

The day before the visits the leadership group prepares for the visits, agreeing how you wish to approach the task, questions to ask etc. The most critical intervention you make during the visits is to ask questions, and provoke discussion. The impact you have is two-fold:

1. What you ask and where you pay attention during your time in the organisation.
2. How you work with the host organisation if you are providing feedback at the end.

The group is split into smaller sub-groups, each sub-group undertaking one stream of interviews. Again, each sub-group will need to agree how they are going to approach their interviews.

Our experience is that this step is critical. Unless you have created some shared meaning as to what the task is, it is difficult to synthesise the findings.

You will be provided with the schedule of interviews and visits that have been arranged by your host organisations.

2. Interviews

You work in pairs as interviewers (except when interviewing the chief executive – which is undertaken by the whole sub-group). Each pair interviews at least four people from the organisation being visited (45 min per interview).

Where logistically possible it is better for the individual interviews to be conducted in the interviewee's own rooms (it gives a better sense of the context in which individuals work). Where there are group conversations (focus type groups) a room where everyone can sit in a circle for a group conversation works best. In addition the host organisation may think that some of the pairs' time would be well spent getting a feel for the work of the organisation by shadowing a person or team for some of the day; or observing an activity or meeting. Those interviewed will not be required to do any preparation. They will also be reassured that the feedback will be in terms of organisational themes and strict individual confidentiality will be preserved.

When interviewing, it is important to stress (and maintain) strict individual confidentiality.

Ask wise questions, not clever ones. Wise questions stimulate answers that can be interpreted, either directly, or in relation to other answers that person gives, or, often most valuably, when looked at across the organisation (when the response changes at different levels in the organisation, the differences between different parts of the org etc.).

Avoid getting sucked into understanding the interviewee's job. You are trying to understand the organisation i.e. what counts, how information flows, who has access to who, how decisions get made, how things get done, how conflict gets handled etc.

Stories and examples are wonderful sources of information. Use them to ground responses (i.e. not can you make a difference?, but tell me about a time when you feel you made a difference …)

Try and notice artefacts, symbols, rituals etc that give some insight into the culture of the organisation (anything from reserved parking, photographs, differential coffee facilities, signposting …)

Try and be as aware as possible of your own assumptions and the conclusions you are drawing. It is easy to decide the answer in the first interview, confirm it in the second and be bored in the third! To get a rich sense of the organisation and all its paradoxes and contradictions; it is helpful to stay open and curious. Take notes, capturing actual words used where possible.

3. Analysis and preparation for presentation

After the interviews you meet in your subgroup to make sense of the visit. You then share your analysis with the rest of the group and collectively prepare your presentation to leaders from the host organisations.

Once again the challenge to the group is to stay open. Do not degenerate into a bun fight over who is right. Share as much direct data as possible. Be open to interpreting your data differently in the light of everyone else's data. Be prepared to modify/ignore the hypotheses you came up with in the planning stage. Struggle to make sense of the whole i.e. what would explain the seemingly contradictory evidence. Remember to record your findings!

In preparing your presentation, remember you were a privileged guest in another organisation. Use the insights you gained with respect, care, compassion and wisdom. Be rigorous in what you present and how you present it.

4. Making your presentation

The presentation is to leaders from the visited organisation. In the presentation you share what you have learnt about how the organisation works, and about your own assumptions and ways of seeing organisations and organisational issues. You can also share what insights the visits gave you into your own organisation. The visits to your host organisation will trigger ideas about your own.

Logistics

In setting up an organisational visit there are a number of steps you need to take:

1. Get consent for the visit and brief the chief executive – you may agree a key questions that you want to explore. Ask for a group to present to at the end of the visit.
2. Get a nominated person from the host organisation to take responsibility for setting up the interviews and sorting out timings/venues/timetable. A sample timetable is provided below, though you could split it over 2 days starting lunchtime day 1 and finishing lunchtime day 2.
3. Get an administrative contact in the host organisation who can sort out car parking, access passes, arrangements for food, arrangements for the presentation session.
4. Provide this briefing to the host organisation.

5. Ask the hosts if they could provide the following:
   - Some background information about the organisation.
   - A meeting room where you as visitors can meet between interviews.
   - Directions for all the activities.
   - Access to tea and coffee and water.
   - Access to lunch.
   - A contact point in case anything goes wrong.
   - A schedule of activities before the visit date.

Outline timetable for visits

09.00–09.30   **Briefing in host organisations** – From chief executive, or senior representative, giving an overview of the organisation and how it works. This should include a brief outline of any challenges and opportunities being faced and the executive's view about how to lead change internally and with partners.

09.30–12.00   **Interviews/discussion groups/observation sessions** – lasting mostly 45 mins max (4 parallel streams)

Time	Session A	Session B	Session C	Session E
09.30–10.15				
10.30–11.15				
11.30–12.15				

Breaks between activities for short debrief discussions (10 mins between each one), and time to travel between activities.

12.15–12.45   **Lunch**

12.30–14.30   **Interviews/discussion groups/observation sessions** (4 parallel streams)

Time	Session A	Session B	Session C	Session E
12.45–13.30				
13.45–14.30				

14.30–15.00   **Whole group meeting with someone from senior management** to clear up any last minute queries/puzzles.

15.00–18.00   Preparation for presentations.

18.00–18.45   Presentation to leaders from visited organisation.

Conversations for possibility

Café Etiquette

FOCUS ON WHAT MATTERS.

CONTRIBUTE YOUR THINKING.

SPEAK YOUR MIND AND HEART.

LISTEN TO UNDERSTAND.

LINK AND CONNECT IDEAS.

LISTEN TOGETHER FOR "INSIGHTS".

AND DEEPER QUESTIONS.

PLAY, DOODLE, DRAW - write on tablecloths.

HAVE FUN!

DARIA MARTIN 2004

The World Café

With thanks to Juanita Brown, Ken Homer and David Isaacs

• Systems • Conversations for possibility • Conversations for connecting intelligence	Conversations to surface possibilities	Minimum of 12 people, no maximum.

> "World Café conversations take us into a new realm, one that has been forgotten in modern individualistic cultures. It is the realm of collective intelligence, of the wisdom we possess as a group that is unavailable to us as individuals. This wisdom emerges in the conversation as we get more and more connected to each other."
>
> Margaret J. Wheatley

The World Café process fosters conversations that matter in groups of 12 to 1200. For thousands of years conversation has been a core process for discovering what we care about, sharing our knowledge, imagining our futures and fostering committed action. World Café conversations build on this long tradition by hosting authentic conversations around core questions that are relevant to the real lives and work of Café participants.

Thousands of people on six continents have experienced World Café dialogues in settings as diverse as large multi-national corporations, small non-profit organisations, government and community-based organisations, health systems, and educational institutions. Lasting from one and half hours to several days, the World Café approach has demonstrated a remarkable capacity to foster meaningful conversations that expand effective knowledge, build relationships, establish trust and create new possibilities for action even among people with no previous history of working together.

The seven principles of the World Café

- Clarify the context.
- Create hospitable space.
- Explore questions that matter.
- Encourage each person's contribution.
- Cross-pollinate and connect diverse perspectives.
- Listen together for patterns, insights and deeper questions.
- Harvest and share collective discoveries.

Some boundaries

The World Café is an appropriate choice you are seeking to:

- Generate input, share knowledge, stimulate innovative thinking, and explore action possibilities around real life issues and questions.
- Engage people in authentic conversation – whether they are meeting for the first time, or are already in established relationships.
- Conduct an in-depth exploration of key strategic challenges or opportunities.
- Deepen relationships and mutual ownership of outcomes in an existing group.
- Create meaningful interaction between a speaker and the audience.
- Work with groups larger than 12 in collaborative dialogue (effective Cafés have been convened with up to 1200).

The World Café is not the most appropriate choice when:

- You are driving toward a previously determined solution or answer.
- You want to convey only one-way information.
- You are making detailed implementation plans.
- You have less than 1.5 hours for the Café (2 hours is much better!).

Set up

Set the room with tables of 30 to 42 inches in diameter with four chairs per table. Size matters! Larger tables will not produce the same quality of intimate conversation and active engagement as smaller ones. We have found that, when requested, small round tables (or even small card tables) have most always been located. If small tables are completely unavailable or if space is at a premium, small conversation clusters have also been used successfully. The number of participants at the table or in the conversation cluster also makes a difference. Four is ideal. Five will work if you are pressed for space, but three provides less diversity of perspectives, while six is too many for everyone to actively contribute.

Creating a warm inviting ambiance is another key success factor. The room should feel more like a café or an informal gathering than sterile conference room presentation. Use chequered tablecloths; candles; flowers; nibbles; music, etc., to make the space as hospitable as possible. Natural lighting, plants, and windows that look out on nature all add a depth that will support your inquiry in surprising ways.

Place two sheets of flipchart paper on top of the tablecloth and at least four different coloured water-based pens so that people can draw on the paper tablecloths, just like in many cafés the world over. If you are working in a conversation cluster, provide large cards and pens for people to note down their insights.

The Café question(s) you are working with (see section on 'Asking meaningful questions') should be prepared and available at the appropriate time to be prominently displayed on a flipchart or blackboard or displayed on an overhead if you are hosting a large gathering.

Welcome people as they enter the room. Ask them to place their bags, laptops and mobile phones off to the side, since they won't need them for a café conversation.

The process

World Café conversations are hosted rather than formally facilitated in the traditional sense. Much like a good dinner host, the job of the overall Café host is to welcome people, put them at ease, share the context and purpose of the gathering and introduce them to the Café process and etiquette. The Café host is also available to answer questions and to support each phase of the process as it unfolds.

Café etiquette

- Focus on what matters.
- Contribute your thinking and experience.
- Speak from the heart.
- Listen to understand.
- Link and connect ideas.
- Listen together for deeper themes, insights and questions.
- Play, doodle, draw – writing on the tablecloth is encouraged!

Let people know that they will have a fixed amount of time to address the question(s) you will be posing in several progressive rounds of conversation and that you will be gently signalling them (often by raising your hand or sounding a small bell) at the end of each round to ask them to change tables. Remind people to use their markers to write, draw and doodle on the paper tablecloths. Often there are very talented people at the Café whose ability to display ideas graphically stimulates new insights. The tablecloth also provides the space to create a "visual memory" of key ideas so they will not be lost.

We have found that it is often helpful to have a "talking object" on the tables. Originally used by indigenous peoples, a talking object can be a stick or stone, a marker or salt shaker— almost anything so long as it can be passed in turn at the table, or placed in the centre where each person can pick up the talking piece as they are moved to speak. There are two aspects to the talking object. The job of the person holding the talking object is to succinctly express their thoughts about the question or issue being explored. The other members' task is to refrain from interrupting, to listen deeply to what the speaker is saying, and to appreciate that perspective of the person holding the talking object, even if divergent from one's own, represents a part of the larger picture which none of us can see by ourselves. Encourage people to link their contributions to those of others and to use the tablecloths to keep noting down key themes, ideas and insights as they emerge.

It is not necessary to use a talking object for every Café round, but it can be a very effective way to slow down the conversation. Ensure that everyone has the opportunity to contribute, and manage people's anxiety about having their say—particularly around controversial questions where it's important to assure that all perspectives are respectfully heard.

In many World Café conversations participants will engage a single question or a set of related questions in three successive "rounds" of dialogue, followed by a period of collective harvesting in a "conversation of the whole". Rounds typically range from 20 to 45 minutes, depending on the available time and nature of the topic. The length can also vary between rounds. At the end of a round, one person remains behind as the table host, while the other members travel to new tables. The table host's job is simply to welcome their travellers and give a very brief overview of the highlights of the previous conversation. Each traveller is then invited to share connections and insights from their own earlier dialogue round. As people rotate to new tables during successive rounds of dialogue, their conversations begin to link and build on each other, emerging patterns and insights reveal themselves, and the wisdom of the group as a whole becomes increasingly visible.

After the third round, the Café host invites participants to harvest their insights in a "conversation of the whole" – town meeting style. Ask participants to share significant learnings, insights, discoveries or the deeper questions that have arisen. Take one initial sharing and ask if others in the room have ideas or insights that link and connect to what was just offered. Keep adding more insights until ideas for that "thread" have been completed. When appropriate, shift the focus and ask for other insights or themes that arose during the Café. Repeat the linking and connecting process until the new threads are woven into the collective tapestry of meaning that is unfolding. This "conversation of the whole" allows the entire room to engage in a reflective discovery process that often results in surprising and useful insights that no one could have anticipated in advance. Be sure to visually capture key themes and ideas if the data are needed for future action planning or follow-up conversations.

Exciting café innovations are being created around the world based on the specific needs of the group who uses it, and the creative implementation of the seven café principles. World Café co-founders Juanita Brown and David Isaacs, with the World Café Community have recently published the first book on the café process entitled: *The World Café: Shaping Our Futures Through Conversations That Matter*. This comprehensive resource contains dozens of real-life stories from people who have hosted cafés on a wide variety of topics, the conceptual underpinnings of the café approach, and a thorough guide to hosting your own World Café dialogues. It is available through amazon.com and most major booksellers. Proceeds are being donated to the World Café Foundation to support the spread of innovative approaches to dialogue on behalf of life-affirming futures.

The World Café also maintains a very useful website and now has an active global online community of inquiry and practice to support Café learning around the world.

Resources

http://www.theworldcafe.com

Brown, J. with Isaacs, D. and the World Café Community (2005) *The World Café: Shaping Our Futures Through Conversations That Matter.* San Francisco: Berrett-Koehler.

Future search

A Future Search conference requires people participating to choose which way the system should go together. There is no escape from the issues that matter, and differences have to be sorted out over the course of the conference. The task is to create direction, and this is held tightly throughout the conference. The process is designed to create new relationships out of old ones, to use difference to create new possibilities for the future, to reach clarity about direction.

This process requires you to get as many people from the system as you can in the room for at least 2 days. This is a large group event, and the room and facilities need to be able to cope with large numbers (see below).

The principles of the design are:

- Use people's own experiences and ideas.
- Everyone has a voice and an equal right to be heard.
- Learn from each other.
- Speak only for yourself.
- Cross-fertilise ideas between groups.
- All information made accessible to all.
- Create the future that we commit to here.

The process goes through six stages:

Stage 1: Review the past from several different perspectives.
Stage 2: Map the present.
Stage 3: Take ownership of the past.
Stage 4: Create a range of future scenarios.
Stage 5: Identify the common ground.
Stage 6: Develop action plans.

Each of the stages above has predictable emotional responses and requirements of the facilitator

Stage	Emotional response	Facilitator's role
Stage One	Concern	Set the task and hold the group to it. Validate the process.
Stage Two	Confusion, anxiety and possibly misery	Stay with it – don't shortcut.
Stage Three	Realisation that 'we' have to do it	Encourage people to take ownership
Stage Four	Hope	Keep it grounded, and focused on the effort still needed
Stage Five	Feet on the ground	Keep focused on real relationships and the patterns already evident
Stage Six	Excitement	Make choices explicit – between replicating old ways in new language or seeking new ways

These need to be recognised in the design of each stage, and in the facilitation of each stage.

A typical Future Search agenda looks like this (though you can condense it):

Day 1, Afternoon
- Review the past
- Map the present, external trends

Day 2, Morning
- Trends continued.
- Focus on the present, owning our actions.

Day 2, Afternoon
- Ideal future scenarios
- Identify common ground

Day 3, Morning
- Common ground continued – confirm
- Action planning

A fuller design can be found in the Future Search field guide, but we can give you some of ideas we have tried here.

Review the past

Timeline: Create a wallpaper gallery (3 strips of lining paper about 12ft long, taped one above another, joining) on which there are 3 horizontal lines equally spaced going the entire length of the wall. Write 'global' on the top one; 'organisational, or the conference issue, or NHS' on the middle one; 'personal' on the bottom one. Date the lines in decades starting at least 30 years ago. Replicate this in the participants' workbooks by creating a page per heading, with boxes for each decade. Ask participants to note memorable events, turning points, major happenings, over the time period in the relevant decade box in their workbook. There is no right or wrong, and you need to discourage conferring. It's a personal exercise. Ask people to transfer their own significant happenings onto the large one on the wall. Once they are all up, ask everyone to look for patterns and trends over time both across the length of each timeline and between the timelines. Break into small groups (max 6 people) and allocate these an area to analyse, to talk about the patterns and trends, illustrating them with their own stories. Each group prepares a 3-minute presentation sharing key themes for the conference as a whole.

Map the present

Mapping external trends shaping this work. Groups work out their views of trends that they think are shaping the current situation (the context to the current) and which could shape the next 10 years. After brainstorming everyone's ideas, each group selects 2 trends that seem most significant to them. In the room is a large blank wall with the issue written at the centre. The groups mind-map their trends on this one wall, each listening to each other's views and adding in their view. Using coloured dots, everyone gets to vote for the ones they think are the most important. Real discussions follow as everyone checks out each other's views in discussion groups.

Take ownership of the past

You need to allocate groups (different from the last exercise) – suggest you do this by labelling tables and giving people badges associated with those labels as they come in.

Each group's task for this session is to make a list on an piece of flipchart paper of what as a group you are proud of in your work in relation to the Conference Issue. Label it: 'Prouds'.

On a separate piece of flipchart paper, each group makes a list of what you are sorry about as a group in your work in relation to the Conference Issue. Label it: 'Sorrys'.

Once you have completed your lists, put them up under the designated signs on the walls (Prouds, Sorrys).

On your tables you will find strips of sticky dots. You have one strip each, to vote for the proudest 'prouds' and sorriest 'sorrys'. Stick your dots against the 'prouds' you think we should be proudest of, and against the 'sorrys' that you think we should be sorriest about. Use your dots as one vote each, with half for the 'prouds' and half for the 'sorrys'. You can use more than one dot for one issue.

The facilitators, with volunteers from the conference, report back the visible results from the dots exercise. The purpose here is some frank ownership and some tolerance of each other in the room. The groups then discuss which of these should be taken into the future – the 'prouds' you want to take with you, the 'sorries' that you need to pay attention to.

Create a range of future scenarios

Back in new mixed groups, people have about 2 hours to prepare their own ideal future scenarios (looking 10 years ahead), as if it was happening now, explaining how the system got there.

Identify a desirable future that is worthy of your efforts and energy.

The future scenario must be one that people want to be part of and do believe in, even if they can't work out how to get there from here. The groups are asked to make their presentation as accessible to everyone as possible, which means being creative in painting a picture (using drama for instance) so that it is not a dry talk, but brings the future scenario alive to those watching. Whilst watching the presentations, the rest of the conference makes notes in their workbooks on visible themes, issues that strike them, things they think need to be in place for these futures to happen.

Once everyone has presented their future, the groups mix again and discuss common themes across all of the scenarios, any ideas about how to get there, and issues that are conflicting/different and unresolved i.e. where there were conflicting future scenarios. These three lists are generated and put up on the wall, by cutting up the flipcharts so that there is one issue per piece of paper. These are posted on the wall in an affinity map (put yours under one that is the same). The lists are merged as they appear up on the wall, looking for definite commonality in each of the list areas (common themes, how to's, unresolved).

Identify the common ground

The conference recognises the unresolved issues and commits to working on the common ground despite these differences. The whole conference reviews the lists again, clarifying the intent in the common statements. Issues can move between lists as we seek to clearly agree what is 'in' the common themes list, and what is meant by what has been written. The groups then work on common underlying conditions that need to be in place for the desired future to happen, selecting 3 that are critical and sharing these with the whole conference.

Develop action plans

Self-selected group work on issues that matter to them. People with ideas for action areas stand up and invite others to join them at their table. As many offers are made as there are ideas in the room. They work on their action and then present what they are planning to do back into the conference as a whole, with details of where and when they will be meeting again so others can join them, and making requests for specific information or help.

In action planning the groups consider:

*   What has to happen next?
*   What resources they need?
*   What do they need to do about information and relationships?
*   What are the principles that underpin how we do this work?
*   Who else do we need to involve?
*   What commitment is the group giving to this work?

These action plans are recorded and circulated straight after the conference closes.

Room set up

You need a venue that can take all the group in one room, seated in groups of 6, and 4ft diameter tables. There needs to be plenty of room to move about around the edge of the tables, and plenty of wall space for putting up the material generated in the room. In addition you need to have natural light; temperature controls; multiple refreshment points; disabled access; PA system. The catering needs to be able to get the entire conference through their food in half an hour – so multiple points; food that can be eaten easily; a lot of serving staff. Tea and coffee should be free-flowing all day. Water should be plentiful. We find it helpful to have healthy snacks available as brain food! There are no breakout rooms; we 'hot house' the issues by keeping the system in the room. Everyone has to confront the difficulties and the opportunities together

Materials

Create a workbook with each exercise/task described in it and space for notes if you want personal reflections in any exercise (e.g. the timelines).

Follow-up

All the conference should have access to progress updates from the action planning groups over the following months/years. This could take many forms and the intent for this should be part of the pre-conference design.

Resources

Weisbord, M.R. & Janoff, S. (1995) *Future Search: An Action Guide to Finding Common Ground in Organisations and Communities*. San Francisco: Berret-Koehler.
http://www.futuresearch.net/. A voluntary world-wide network offering public, non-profit and NGO future search processes and training for whatever people can afford.

Conversational conferences

With thanks to Julian Pratt

- Autopoiesis
- Social systems

Maximise the potential of networks, and the possibility of expertise in a system.

For conferences of medium to large groups

We have all experienced conferences that revolve around expert presentations, where part of what's said is useful for context, and we find out about some things we think we'll try out in our own patch. In terms of using the expertise in the room, they are dismally ineffective. If our focus is on implementation – i.e. changing our practice, then a more interactive, involving learning conference is required. The conversational conference draws on the benefits from traditional conferences and large group interventions.

> "Conversational conferences:
> - Are designed to provide the space and tie for participants to learn from and with each other.
> - Use conversations and personal experiences to build relationships and bring about changes in understanding.
> - Value the expertise of participants as a resource for change as well as the expertise offered by 'outside experts'.
> - Give rise to changed understanding and behaviour, and support local innovation and changes in working practices."
>
> Pratt (2003)

The practice

Firstly the design needs to reflect the needs of the participants. A pre-conference design group meets to identify the issues that need to be prepared, and the needs of the group. In order to support the small groups in the work, you need to provide a workbook that takes each participant through the conference (both in terms of instructions for the exercises, clear questions for the conversations, breaks and how to form the groups). As the groups are self-facilitated, the pre-conference design group can help with providing clear unambiguous questions for the group work. You can't manage the outcome of the conversations but you can be clear about the principles of how to work in small groups, so that everyone's voice gets heard.

The conference moves between presentation, small group conversation and large group conversation (present ideas; make sense of what's been heard; share learning and insights). In addition 'hot topics' can be identified early (at the beginning) in the conference from participants, and space given to working on those topics during the day (be it controversial or difficult issues for discussion, or interest areas for sharing practice).

For the presentations, the speakers will need a brief about the conference, and about the expectations of them providing a presentation that sets the context to the questions the groups will work on.

From here on, the role of the facilitator is to model the principles of the design (including managing people who take up too much air time in the whole conference conversation); and keep the conference to time. In addition you may choose to work with a strategic illustrator to capture the work of the conference over the duration.

Set-up

All the small group conversations happen within groups of 6–8 people seated around 4-ft diameter round tables. The rest of the venue is as described in the section on 'Design and facilitation'.

References, reading, resources

Pratt, J., Plamping, D., Gordon, P. (2003) Conversational conferences: from ideas to action. *British Journal of Health Care Management*, **9**, 3, pp 98–103.

Conversations to determine
values/principles/agreements

Gathering stories

• Social systems • Dissipative systems • Autopoiesis • Cognition	Uncovering lived values in a system, system's identity	Work in groups of 6, as many as system requires (we have worked with >100).

"… any event retold from life which appeared to carry some meaning, however small, is a story"

Reason & Hawkins (1988)

"When we start telling stories we gave our lives a new dimension of meaning – apprehension-comprehension."

Ben Okri

Telling stories is a rich way of uncovering the living values and the identity of your organisation/department/team. By listening to stories of meaningful memorable events/situations in the workplace, you will hear the underlying assumptions; expectations; the ways of doing things round here. By listening to how these stories trigger other stories in other people, you will hear how stories get interpreted through the underlying lens that the organisation has on the world (its identity). A storytelling workshop as described here helps you see what matters to the group who are telling stories, as they go about their work i.e. what governs their behaviours (what matters). You can see how congruent these stories are with your organisation/department/team's espoused values.

To gather stories in a workshop it helps if the participants do some pre-work, gathering a few stories of their own. Here is how they go about it.

The practice

Collecting stories for a small workshop or storytelling meeting

You might like to organise a storytelling event/meeting/workshop locally, or within your own team. Here is how you can go about collecting some stories to start you off at the workshop. At the meeting you might want to agree Chatham House rules (the issues can be discussed outside the group but are not attributable). Certainly some ground rules should be agreed about confidentiality before you start the pre-meeting work of collecting stories.

Your story

Firstly – your own story. Think of an event/situation in which you have been involved in your work, in the past 2 years (as a member of staff or as a user) and which has really made an impact on you. It might have altered your views of how you should go about your job; it might have affirmed a view you passionately held; it might have affected how you think about the employing organisation or your own behaviour. It should be something at the forefront of your memory, and something that you are willing to share with others.

Once you have remembered a 'defining moment' for you, write it down. This is for your own record only.

Someone else's story

Now choose someone who will be able to tell you their story without feeling intimidated, or wanting to hide any of the details. Perhaps it could be a work colleague, or a friend who is a staff member or user, or someone who volunteers from within your organisation.

We have found that people have really enjoyed telling their stories and being listened to. It seems rare for people to share the important moments/experiences that have shaped their thinking and actions. Stories usually last only a couple of minutes. This is not a time-consuming task, but you do need to give it your full attention. You should:

1. Explain to your storyteller that you want to listen to their story and that you will be telling it at an event to a small group of service staff and users, but that it will not be attributed to them.
2. Ask them to tell you about an event in which they have been involved in the last few years and has made a lasting impression on them. It can be a 'good' or 'bad' story. It should be easy for them to recall and could be about anything from a story about an incident involving a patient or relative, about a relationship with a colleague, about something they fought for. The story can be about something seemingly quite small, or a major incident. Whichever it is, we are not looking for anecdotes, rather for tales about events that carry some meaning for the storyteller. Something they won't forget.
3. Take notes of the story and tell it back to the 'teller', to make sure that you have captured the essence of the story.

4. You may find that the story you have been told triggers a memory of yours – something similar from your own experience, or a direct contradiction from your own experience. You may want then to share your story with the other person. If not, then at least jot some notes to remind you of your 'reply' story.
5. Then ask the storyteller what their story means to them and what impact it has had on them, and take notes. Again these notes are for your own use to help you remember at the workshop. Please make sure that after the workshop you destroy the notes you have made.

The workshop

You will need 6 participants. We suggest if you are doing this for an organisation, that you use groups of 6 and run them all in parallel, gathering themes as you go along (see 'Café process'). At this stage we are going to outline how to do the process for a group of 6 working together from 09.00 to 14.00.

Set–up

You will need a room that can comfortably seat your group in circles of chairs (for 6), and flipcharts and pens for the summaries or to capture ideas.

15 mins   Explain the reason for the work, and why we are doing it like we are. Introduce yourselves. Explore joint expectations.

30 mins   Explain how you are going to work during the workshop and do a dummy round telling stories of their journeys here today.

Start the storytelling.

The process for stories is as follows:

• Everyone writes their (defining moment) story down (then they don't lose them, and they don't get remade by other stories as the day goes on).
• Someone tells their (defining moments) story ("I remember when…") without interpreting it.
• Everyone has a few minutes to think about connections to anything in their own work experience (internal sense-making and interpretation) – quietly and on their own – and to write it down. Ask for connecting/contrasting stories – and for that story to be told without the storyteller explaining the connection/contrast. "I have a similar story …" " I have had

a different experience …" They tell their similar/contrasting stories until their stories are exhausted or the time is up for this section.

- If participants get stuck ask the group for a volunteer to tell the story back (from this you 'expose' the volunteer's interpretation of the story) – ask the group how they have heard the 2 stories, the original and when it was repeated.
- Having exhausted this round, start again, having a break for coffee every 2 rounds (15 mins).
- Start again at the beginning – each round to last half an hour.
- If the process gets boring, and the group is willing, get the telling back to change shape, or the initial story to change shape – draw it, tell it as a poem.
- At 3.15pm we have a go at the 'whole' – ask them to make up a story that captures all the parts (facilitate this by neutral questions); get them to write individual poems; get them to draw a picture of the day.
- Finally let them make comments on the day and make interpretations if they are burning to do so, and remind them of the what next …

Break for lunch at 12.15pm–12.45pm. Coffee and tea to be plentiful throughout, as well as snacks (fruit). Room layout, as informal as possible, comfy chairs arranged in the round. Small coffee table only.

Timetable for a small group

09.00	Intros
09.15	Explain process and do a dummy run
09.45	Storyline 1
10.15	Storyline 2
10.45	Coffee
11.00	Storyline 3
11.30	Storyline 4
12.00	Lunch
12.15	Storyline 5
12.45	Storyline 6
13.15	Whole day story
13.45	Comments/thoughts and what next
14.00	Close.

Ideally go for 6 stories – it is possible to do 8 and the minimum is 3.

References, resources, reading

Malby, B. & Pattison, S. (1999) *Living Values in the NHS. Stories from the NHS's 50th year*. London: King's Fund.

Allan, J., Fairtlough, G. & Heinzed, B. (2001) *The Power of the Tale. Using Narratives for Organisational Success*. Chichester: John Wiley & Sons Ltd.

http://www.nelh.nhs.uk/knowledge_management/km2/storytelling_toolkit.asp

Reason, P. & Hawkins, P. (1988) Storytelling as inquiry. In: P. Reason (ed.) *Human Inquiry in Action*. London: Sage.

Inquiring into promising practices

With thanks to Myron Rogers

• Cognition • Systems • Social systems	Organisational inquiry into making most of what is promising internally.	Whole system. We have worked with >100 in the room.

This inquiry is based on the premise that every system works to some degree. In this session your task is to uncover what's working in your system, and why, so that we can understand the conditions that support more of this kind of work in the system.

The process is energising. It requires us to listen and converse differently. In organisations we are used to listening to problems and being required to find answers. In discussion we jump into decisions and actions, moving from one problem to another.

This inquiry requires us to listen for the best about people in their workplace. We try to find out about things at their best – the successes – so that we can infuse more of this in the individual and organisation's activity.

For this exercise you work in groups of 6 (3 pairs from different departments). You each take turns (in pairs) to take on the 3 roles of interviewer, interviewee, and observer.

Set-up

Circles of chairs for 6 people. No tables. Post-It notes or labels for writing up each condition. A large blank wall covered with lining paper for the 'Affinity' work.

The role of the storyteller

Your role is to tell the story of any 'promising practice' in your team. A promising practice is any practice that achieves results congruent with when you see the system working at its best. So, it may be a practice that increases connections between teams, departments, partners in pursuit of linked goals. It may be a practice that overcomes organisational barriers to effective work. It may be a practice that presented a new possibility for how to organise work. It is likely to be a practice that created new capacity in a team or group and created different results. The practice is likely to have achieved success, though not always. Sometimes innovative approaches fail, but teach us something worth capturing in the process. Often people feel they are doing extraordinary or different work – but again, not always. Sometimes new ways of working come with frustration or resistance. Overall, you're looking at your recent work to find evidence that supports new ways of working together that could create more effectiveness, or could create greater capacity for development, and could bring about better results.

As you take a few minutes to think about your story, here are some elements to consider:

- What was the practice intended to do?
- What actually happened? What were the outcomes for the team, the organisation, partners, and the community?
- Who was involved in this (populations as well as individuals)?
- What is the promise of the practice? If this practice was adopted more broadly, what impact would it have?
- Why did you choose this work in this way?
- What evidence do you have that this is a Promising Practice?
- What have you learned?

Try not to be too humble about this, enjoy telling the story, and try to work through what it was that enabled you to make this promising practice happen.

The role of the interviewer

So, to start the interviews, the interviewer needs to introduce the process of the interview, saying that the interview will focus on the promising practices in the interviewee's work life (stories of when things have been at their best). You will be listening and looking for the instances when the person you are interviewing 'comes alive' to gain a better understanding between you of what gives the interviewee's vitality and success.

Start by asking for a story about "A time when you felt you and your team were working at your best…." Probe deeply and intently to get to what they did and thought and felt. Use open-ended questions such as:

- 'Why do you think that?'
- 'Who else is involved?'

- 'What do you think he/she would say, if they were here?'
- 'What is the most important thing?'
- 'Have you been in this sort of situation before?'
- 'What did you do then?'
- 'How were the outcomes different?'

Then ask about the conditions that supported the times when the interviewee felt like this, what was it about self, team and the organisation that they worked in? Probe for specifics. If they say – "we were allowed to take a risk" – what do they mean by 'allowed'? How is that different from other times at work? So ask questions that get deeper into the interviewee's answers. Try to expand the member's understanding of the practice, with questions like:

- 'How do you know that?'
- 'How is this different? (from other work and the ways things are done round here).'
- 'What about the relationships (in the team, across the organisation, with partners, with the community).'
- 'What about the quality and use of information?'
- 'What are your hypotheses about what was going on?'

The role of the observers

The role of the observer is to listen for the conditions underpinning the interviewee's story of their promising practice (the interviewee's story of success/ achievement and vitality in their work) and make notes of these. Your will then share your interpretations with the interviewer and interviewee at the end of the interview, and as a group come to some conclusions about the conditions that enabled the interviewee to work at their best. By conditions we mean anything that was fundamental to this promising practice taking place (e.g. taking a risk and what enabled that to happen; a particular supportive relationship; a new policy; personal drive). We expect that for each promising practice there will be multiple conditions that enabled it to happen. You need to be really clear what was critical for the interviewee.

20 mins	Interview 1
5 mins	As a group identify the key conditions for this interviewee (see above).
20 mins	Interview 2
5 mins	As a group identify the key conditions for this interviewee (see above).

20 mins   Interview 3

5 mins   As a group identify the key conditions for this interviewee (see above).

Put each different underlying condition you have identified for all your stories on an individual label, giving as good a description of that condition as you can. For instance if you decide that communication was key then say between whom, and why that was so critical for your stories.

You then 'affinity' your labels. Basically, you put each condition up on the wall, where possible underneath one that is already up there, that seems to you to be the same. If you can't find one the same, then start a new column.

Emerging themes

We look for and agree the common themes.

Identifying guiding principles and agreements

- Emergence

| Identify system principles and agreements | Large group working in the system. |

This exercise is for a large group of people working in one defined system (e.g. an organisation – local authority; NHS Trust) to determine their guiding principles for the whole. You need to determine the groups that will work together. We find that 'home' groups that best represent people's work experience i.e. teams/departments is the most productive starting place.

For this exercise you work in home groups to come up with the guiding principles and the associated agreements we need across the system in order to be an effective organisation.

You need to come up with up to 4 principles. Please put each one on a separate sheet of flipchart paper. Each one must be evidenced by an example of how that principle works in practice now, or could help with something currently going on in the system.

By guiding principles we mean simple rules of thumb that will govern the way we work together. For each guiding principle you need to identify the agreements that need to be in place (i.e. what we need to do to make the principle happen).

For instance you might have a principle that:

All information is open and available to all.
The agreement could be that everyone would make information available to the whole organisation.

Or

We will aim for agreement and stick to it.
The agreement here could be that if there are different views about an issue that they get heard, and that there is a process for working through divergent/conflicting views, that everyone agrees to.

Or

We need feedback mechanisms to link individual and organisational learning, and to make sense of how we are doing.
The agreement here could be that all meetings would have processes for feedback and review

Once you have come up with your guiding principles and agreements, you need to be able to 'sell' them to the others in the room in 3 minutes. So be clear about what difference they will make and how they will help you do your work in the future.

Each principle is displayed on the wall, grouping 'like' ones together. A few volunteers then make headings for the groups and report back to the whole group.

Timetable

09.30–09.45	Instructions
09.45–09.50	Get into home groups
09.50–10.45	Decide your guiding principles and agreements
10.45–11.10	Break
11.10–11.40	Marketplace – everyone has 3 minutes (depending on numbers of groups) to sell their ideas to the rest of the conference.
11.40–12.00	Whole groups dialogue and display all in the room.
12.00–12.30	Affinity

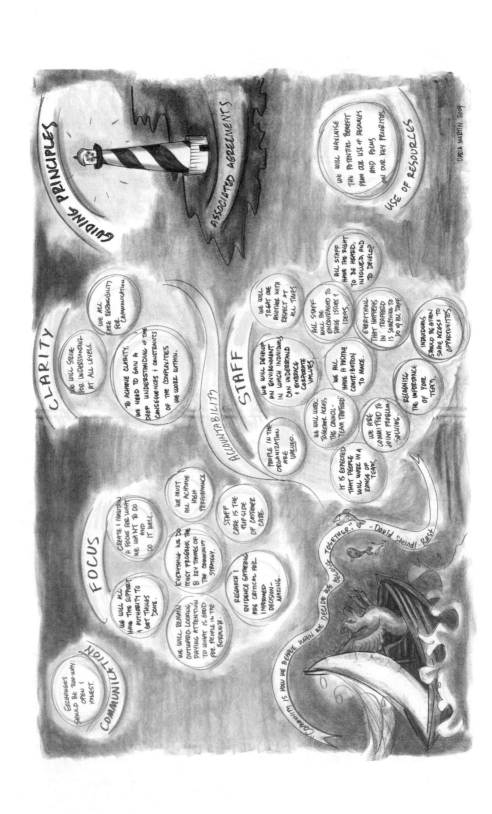

GUIDING PRINCIPLES

ASSOCIATED AGREEMENTS

USE OF RESOURCES

We will maximise the potential benefit from all use of resources and focus on our key priorities.

CLARITY

We will strive for understanding at all levels.

We all take responsibility for communication.

To achieve clarity, we need to gain a deep understanding of the consequences & constraints of the complexities we work within.

ACCOUNTABILITY

STAFF

We will treat one another with respect at all times.

We will develop an environment in which individuals can understand & embrace corporate values.

All staff will be encouraged to raise issues & ideas.

All staff have the right to be heard, involved, and to develop.

Everything that happens is trapped. Is something to do w/ all staff.

We all have a positive contribution to make.

Individuals should be given share access to opportunities.

People in the organization are valued.

We will work together across the council. Team threshold.

We are committed to joint problem solving.

Recognise the importance of your team.

It is expected that people will work in a range of teams.

FOCUS

Create & maintain a focus for what we want to do and do it well.

We must all achieve high performance.

We will all have the support & authority to get things done.

Everything we do must progress the 8 key themes of the community strategy.

Staff care is the flip-side of customer care.

We will remain outward looking, paying attention to what is good for people in the borough.

Research & evidence gathering are critical for informed decision-making.

COMMUNICATION

Exchanges should be two-way: open & honest.

"Community is how we behave when we decide we belong together." - David Steindl-Rast

DARIA MARTIN 2009

Conversations for action

OPEN SPACE

Whoever comes are the RIGHT PEOPLE

Whenever it starts IS THE RIGHT TIME

Whatever happens IS THE ONLY THING THAT COULD HAVE

When it's over, IT'S OVER

THE LAW of TWO FEET:

If at any time you are not learning or contributing USE YOUR TWO FEET to MOVE somewhere ELSE.

DARIA MARTIN 2004

Open space

With thanks to Harrison Owen, the originator of Open Space Practice

- Emergence
- Systems
- Multiple perspectives

Process for a system to work on key complex question, where there are diverse views.

For as much of the system as can be present min 20, no max (we have worked with hundreds).

Open Space[1] is a self-organising practice that enables all kinds of people to work on what matters to them. The outcome is unknowable. The practice is a key set of organising principles. It requires no facilitation at all beyond setting up the process and the dialogue at the end.

Open Space invites people in a system to take responsibility for issues they care about with others who also have energy for that issue.

In essence participants create their own agenda, run discussion groups and action plan around the things that matter to them, in relation to a key organising complex question.

The process can run from half a day to 3 days, for small groups or incredibly large groups. It has a number of features:

1. It enables multiple voices and perspective to be heard.
2. It goes where there is energy in the system through conversations that matter, and harnesses that for productive action.
3. It generates action quickly.
4. There is no way that this action can be predicted prior to the Open Space.

Open space works best where there is a key complex question that generates energy in the system (conflict, passion, impatience); where there are multiple and diverse views; where they system itself needs to be engaged to reach action.

Most importantly the process gets to documented visible agreements about action fast, in a way that makes the most of everyone's contribution, and that is fun!

---

[1] Created by Harrison Owen in 1985.

The design is based on the following assumptions:

1. Conversation is work.
2. The system knows what to do.
3. The energy is in the system to take the right action.

And is organised using the following principles (described in more detail below)

1. Whoever comes are the right people
2. Whatever happens is the only thing that could have.
3. Whenever it starts is the right time.
4. When it's over, it's over.

And one law – The law of two feet.

The practice

Firstly find the key energising question that embodies the complex issue with which the system is grappling (see section on Asking meaningful questions).

Identify all the people engaged in the system described by the question. Select whom you are going to invite proportionally to their presence in the system.

Invite people from the system to come to a day/more to work on this question.

Set up the space

You need a large main meeting room, and several breakout rooms, all with flipcharts, pens and a circle of chairs.

In the main meeting room set the chairs in a circle, or concentric circles (with aisles so that people can get into the middle of the room). Check whether you need a PA system.

On one wall cover the wall with lining paper (at least 3 metres high, 9 metres long – depending on the size of the group). Mark the paper into squares (see chart), and put up strips of masking tape. Cut up squares of paper about ¼ of flipchart size, and put these in the centre of the circle of chairs on the floor, along with several marker pens.

Make sure the question you are asking is prominently displayed in all the rooms along with posters that show the rules for Open Space (see below), and the feedback headings:

1. Topic
2. Who came
3. Issues discussed
4. Action planned.
5. Contact details.

The Open Space agenda chart

Example times	Rm 1	Rm 2	Rm 3	Rm 4	Rm 5	Rm 6
10.00–10.45						
Coffee						
11.15–12.00						
Lunch						
13.00–13.45						
13.45–14.30						
Tea						
15.00–15.45						

As people come into the room, welcome them and ask them to take their seats. When you are ready to begin, explain the process. We start with the purpose of the day (restate the question), and that every change starts with people gathering together in a circle to talk about what matters to them. Show the people gathered the agenda, and explain the process for the day:

1. How to create the agenda
2. The rules and principles of Open Space.
3. How to create a record of your meetings

Ask the group to be silent and to think about the question. Invite anyone who would like to work on an aspect of that question/who cares about an issue to come into the centre of the room, and tell the whole group the topic (not a lengthy explanation, just the highlights, checking that it has been understood). They then write the topic on a piece of paper, put their name on it and put it up on the agenda wall in one of the allocated slots.

This goes on until everyone who has an issue/topic has put it on the wall. Everyone then gets up and signs up for the topics they want to take part in.

If people want to go to several that are running at the same time, then the whole group is engaged in sorting the agenda to make the most of everyone's energy.

Once an agreed agenda is up on the wall, the timings are confirmed, and the meetings begin.

At the closing session all the meeting hosts bring their report sheets, and read out the action they are going to take as a group with dates, times and contact details. There is then a closing discussion as a whole about key themes; what happened; the process itself, and what the whole community has achieved.

These report sheets are typed up (if possible during coffee/lunch/tea) and circulated to the whole group ideally as they leave the event, if not within the next day.

How it works – the rules and principles

The **'Law of two feet'** is simply this: if at any time you find yourself in any situation where you are neither learning nor contributing, use you two feet and move to some place more to your liking. Such a place might be another group, or even outside into the sunshine.

It means you take responsibility for what you care about – standing up for that and using your own two feet to move to whatever place you can best contribute and/or learn.

Four principles apply to how you navigate in open space:

1. Whoever comes are the right people.
   Whoever is attracted to the same conversation are the people who can contribute most to that conversation – because they care. So they are exactly the ones – for the whole group – who are capable of initiating action.

2. Whatever happens is the only thing that could have.
   This principle keeps us focused on the here and now, rather than getting distracted by all the 'could haves', or 'should haves' or 'if onlys'.

3. When it starts is the right time.
   Creativity happens in its own time, not when the clock says it should. Our task is to make our best contribution and enter the flow of creativity when it starts.

4. When it's over, it's over.

   Do what you want to do; when it's done, then stop. Don't spin it out to fill the time. Ask: "is it over?" and if it is, go on to the next thing you have passion for.

References, resources, reading

www.openspaceworld.com

http://www.openspaceworld.org/wiki/wiki/wiki.cgi?AboutOpenSpace – the process explained and described; other people's stories.

Owen, H. (1997) *Open Space Technology: A User's Guide.* 2nd edn. San Francisco: Berrett-Koehler.

Owen, H. (2000) *The Power of Spirit: How Organizations Transform.* San Francisco: Berrett-Koehler.

Real time strategic change

With thanks to Robert Jacobs

• Systems • Social • Emergence	Designing sustainable change	Large group –as many from the system as you can get.

Real-time strategic change brings together recognition of patterns of the past and exploration and agreement about future direction, into commitments as to what needs to be done differently in order to get there, and plans to make those changes. The focus is on current reality as the basis for planning and change, and the wisdom of the large group to work simultaneously on team, group, organisation and system-wide change that positions the whole organisation for success now and in the future. It's a 'both/and' approach, rather than an 'either/or' approach, in that it makes the most of what works now, and redesigns for the future. It supports people working in their own team and working for the good of the whole organisation; it enables an internal and an external focus; it makes the most of the benefits of participation across the whole, and direction for specific issues.

The process of RTSC is a set of principles in action that allow the organisation to change sustainably. In effect these principles can be used to design change for many issues the organisation is working on.

The design of RTSC work is based on the belief that:

(a) The entire organisation and its stakeholders/partners need to be involved for meaningful real time change to happen.
(b) Multiple perspectives are critical to the success of real time change – the diversity of everyone's views has to be shared and heard
(c) This has to be set in the context of reality – a shared, informed and mapped past, present and future.

This translates into the principles that underpin all RTSC design shown opposite.

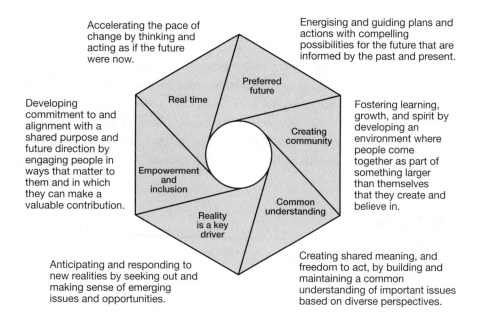

Accelerating the pace of change by thinking and acting as if the future were now.

Energising and guiding plans and actions with compelling possibilities for the future that are informed by the past and present.

Developing commitment to and alignment with a shared purpose and future direction by engaging people in ways that matter to them and in which they can make a valuable contribution.

Fostering learning, growth, and spirit by developing an environment where people come together as part of something larger than themselves that they create and believe in.

Anticipating and responding to new realities by seeking out and making sense of emerging issues and opportunities.

Creating shared meaning, and freedom to act, by building and maintaining a common understanding of important issues based on diverse perspectives.

Source: Holma & Devane (1999) *The Change Handbook*

Real time strategic change principles

The pre-conditions for engaging in RTSC are that:

- the need for change is now;
- the leadership is both open to different ways of working and ideas for what to do, and is committed to sharing power across the organisation;
- the organisation is seeking sustainable lasting change – not a quick fix.

Typically organisations engaged in the RTSC approach, work with design teams to design a change process, congruent with the principles (by using the above hexagon), that:

(a) Scopes possibilities
(b) Develops and aligns leadership.
(c) Creates organisational congruence.

You will find that the design team needs to use other practices such as mapping intended and unintended consequences, as part of their design process.

One key part of this work is the RSTC event which uses the practices of dialogue; storytelling, large-group conversation; contextualisation; feedback

133

to engage people in the above process. These events should be part of a wider designed change effort, not a stand-alone, one-off.

You can use the practice for smaller groups or for larger groups, but here we describe an example practice for a large group, where you are bringing as many people as possible from the organisation or system into the room for the whole event (which can take place over 3 days). The process works for 500 and for 3,000. For more information about integrating RTSC into your organisation's development, please read the chapter in *The Change Handbook* (see references below).

RTSC event

The event is designed using processes that enable:

1. Multiple perspectives.
2. Participation.
3. Access to information.
4. Learning.
5. Reality checks.

It goes through stages of:

*   Check-in.
*   Clarity of purpose and expectations.
*   The Context for change.
*   Organisational diagnosis of the present.
*   Mapping the future.
*   Possibilities for change.
*   Organisational norms.

In all of these the process moves between the individual, the small group, the whole group and back again, persistently working through these scales.

No event is ever the same as any other. Facilitators need to adapt and create a design that works with the issues in the room.

An example process could go like this (with thanks to Jane Jacobs):

1. **Check-In**

    In small groups, around round tables, beginning by using the first principles of dialogue – listening to each other's stories.

2. **Expectations**

   a) in the same small groups, what will make the time together here worth-while for the individuals present. Why is that? What has been happen-ing – what are you proud of, what has frustrated you? Look for themes and differences as a group, and post these up on the display boards.

   b) At this stage the leadership group from the organisation is up front, and looks at the themes and provides its own view of challenges; vision for the future; where the organisation needs top focus.

   c) What did we hear? – again in small groups (at new tables now) a dis-cussion about what was heard, and time to make sense of it. A short session follows posting questions for the leadership group and the RTSC event to cover.

3. **Organisational diagnosis** – What's going on now?

   a) Tables are given topics and asked to tell stories and list what they are glad/sad/mad about in relation to this topic over the past year. The top-ics can be like these:
      - Our purpose.
      - Decision making.
      - Relationships in teams and across parts of the organisation.
      - Recruitment and retention.
      - Working with conflict.
      - Policies and procedures.
      - Rewards and recognition.
      - Learning and development.
      - Information (access to, relevance).
      - Budgeting.
      - Governance.

   b) Voting on the gladdest glads, saddest sads, maddest mads. Everyone has 2 votes for each of these per topic (sticky dots). The topics with their lists of glad/sad/mads are put up and everyone reads the whole and votes.

   c) This is followed by a brief report out.

4. **Mapping the future** – This comprises 3 separate parts:

   a) The content expert to contextualise the future – ask an analyst, or someone that concentrates on trends that could impact on your organisation over the next 5–10 years, or a current leader in the organisation, or someone from outside that can articulate the context well.

   b) The customer – user. Find a way of bringing the customer's perspective into the room – using an 'expert' customer; or ask a theatre group to interview customers and play back a story using all the material they gather.

   c) The expertise in the room – discussions across groups about the possibilities for the future, using the context generated so far. This could be a mini-café type process (see Café section).

   The discussions about future are captured during a large group dialogue – this is the time where a strategic illustrator can be really helpful.

5. **Possibilities for change**

   a) A catalytic conversation taking place in front of the whole event. A small group of people discuss changes they have implemented in the organisation, explaining why, how they did it, what worked and what didn't, what they learned. This can also take place on tables of 6 using the promising practices approach (see section on 'Promising practices').

   b) The event breaks up into functional groups (departments/teams) where they work out what they think needs to be different and who else they will need to do this. They write Valentines to each other like this:

   To.............(specific group)
   These are the things we need you to do differently in the future so we can better meet our customer's needs.
   From ....(Function group).

   These Valentines are circulated, read, read again, responded to thoughtfully and non-defensively. Prepare a report to the whole event detailing briefly the key themes you heard and your non-defensive response.

6. **Organisational norms** (How things are done round here – the simple rules of thumb we operate by).

   a) Mixed table brainstorm the norms that underpin work now, indicating whether it is helpful, whether it makes it harder to reach our goals, or whether it has no impact at all.

   b) Circulate and look at everyone else, then go back to your table and identify one negative norm that really must change, replacing it with a new helpful norm. All these changes are called out in a marketplace to convince others. This is followed by a whole group conversation about the knock-on effects of the changes. Some sorting takes place in the whole to identify the agreed changes to the norms.

7. **Organisation strategy revisited**

   a) If you have an organisational strategy, this is the time to run it against the following:
      • What we've learnt here about how change happens
      • What we have learnt about the norms
      • What we have learnt about the future.

   From this discussion mark out what you agree with; disagree with and what changes you recommend (explaining your rationale).

   b) Leadership turnaround on strategy – this can be the leadership group and/or the design team for the strategy. The strategy gets re-written in real time here, identifying what has changed and why. This is usually overnight.

8. **Preferred future**

   a) This process identifies what success would look like if the strategy worked, and how we'd know. Groups describe how they would feel, what they would see, what they would hear if they have achieved the strategy. These are put on Post-its and an affinity wall created (put your Post-it below one that is the same/similar, if there is none like yours, create a new line).

   b) Rooms are assigned to themes from the affinity wall and the group in the room is given the Post-its from their theme. The group writes a preferred future statement based on the themes; identifies the things happening now in the organisation that will help move towards that future; identifies the things that will make it difficult; brainstorms a list of actions needed; agrees the three most important ones. These are posted in the main room for all to read.

9. **Action planning**

Everyone returns to their home team, and discusses the implications for their own work and team's work, agreeing now on what you will now do differently and how you will bring the rest of your team on board. These agreements are reported to the main event. The actions will have timetables, which will be followed up after the event.

10. **Evaluation**

This event usually takes place over 3 days. Evaluation is important at the end of each day, and the beginning of the next (this one concentrating more on what has settles overnight). A final evaluation of the whole undertaken visibly closes the event.

Set-up

You need a venue that can take the whole group around tables (4ft) in groups of 6. The attendance should reflect the whole organisation, and all levels of staff. The venue also needs break-out rooms for team-based discussions; plenty of wall space and natural light; catering facilities that can cope with large numbers.

We strongly advise working with a strategic illustrator to capture the work, particularly the whole group discussions.

Doing more with RTSC

As with all practices and principles, RTSC has been evolving. In it is what the originator Robert Jacobs calls its 'third generation'. It has brought further innovation to the world of RTSC through defining the six fundamental principles as polarities whose tensions need to be managed well in order to achieve accelerated, sustainable change. The better these polarities are managed, the faster and more sustainable the change you achieve. For more information see Robert Jacob's website.

References, resources and reading

Jacobs, R. (1997) *Real Time Strategic Change. How to Involve an Entire Organization in Fast and Far-Reaching Change.* San Francisco: Berrett-Koehler.

Jacobs, R. & McKeown, F. (1999) Real time strategic change. In Holman, P. & Devane, T. (eds) *The Change Handbook: Group Methods for Shaping the Future.* San Francisco: Berrett-Koehler.

Jacobs, R. & Mc Keown, F. (1999) *Collaborating for Change: Real Time Strategic Change.* San Francisco: Berrett-Koehler.

http://www.rwjacobs.com

Appreciative interviewing

- Cognition
- Autopoiesis
- Social

To focus on what works; uncover the conditions that support what works.

Work in 3s. These groups work in parallel. Can be for a small team and for a whole system. We have done this with >100 in the room.

Appreciative interviewing is described as part of a wider process called 'appreciative inquiry'. We do not cover this here, as we have found that the interviewing piece to be the most beneficial part of the whole process. For more about appreciative inquiry please see the website below.

Essentially Appreciative Inquiry is based on the premise that all systems work to some degree. Our approach is that it is the leader's role to uncover where and how the system is working; focus energy and attention on understanding why and how it works; and support the conditions that are enabling the system to work well.

We describe appreciative interviewing here in relation to a specific inquiry about corporate working, by people working within a department/directorate. The purpose here is both to uncover 'what works' and also to appreciate what it takes to lead at corporate level. You can use appreciative interviewing across departments/sectors that need to work together where there are assumptions about the 'other' that may be unhelpful. You can also use it in teams to focus your energy on amplifying where the teams works well.

We use the term 'appreciate' here in the affective. It does not mean 'like' or focusing on positive scenarios – it literally means appreciating the conditions that support things working round here (which could be how conflict is handled for instance).

The example below is an exemplar. You can adapt it to your needs. The next piece of work once you have undertaken interviews is to analyse and interrogate the conditions to see what that might mean for how you organise.

What works at corporate level

The purpose of this interview is to find out how working at corporate level (on behalf of and in service to the whole PCT) is different or not from working at department/directorate level, and what conditions support successful corporate working in this PCT. You do this by asking someone working at corporate level to tell you a story/stories of times when that feel they have worked well on behalf of and in service to the whole PCT.

We are asking you to do this using a specific technique – appreciative interviewing. The premise of this is that all systems work to some degree, and our role as leaders and managers is to uncover what's working and make more of those moments. At present the NHS seems locked in a cycle of identifying endlessly what's not working, and trying to fix it with varying success, in the process throwing up more unintended problems that need fixing. This process focuses on what is working now, and how to amplify the impact of this across the PCT.

Firstly you need to find a partner, and then find 2 people (staff member or non-executive member) working at corporate level (i.e. the board, executive, PEC) to interview. For the interviews you take turns acting as interviewer, and as observer. You will need about half an hour for each interview.

The interview process

So, to start the interviews the interviewer needs to introduce the process of the appreciative interview, saying that the interview will focus on the times in the interviewees work at corporate level when things have been at their best. Explain that this is to help learn about what it takes to work well at corporate level.

You will be listening and looking during the interview for the instances when the person you are interviewing 'comes alive' to gain a better understanding between you of what gives the interviewee vitality and success.

Start by asking for a story about: "A time when you felt you were working at your best at corporate level on behalf of/in service to the PCT as a whole…." Probe deeply and intently to get to what they did and thought and felt.

Use open-ended questions such as:

- 'Why do you think that?'
- 'Who else is involved?'
- 'What do you think he/she would say, if they were here?'
- 'What is the most important thing?'
- 'Have you been in this sort of situation before?
- 'What did you do then?'
- 'How were the outcomes different?'

Then ask about the conditions that supported the times when the interviewee felt like this. Use questions like:

- 'How do you know that?'
- 'How is this different? (from other work and the ways things are done round here).'
- 'What about the relationships (in the team, across the organisation, with partners, with the community).'
- 'What about the quality and use of information?'
- 'What are your hypotheses about what was going on?'

Some of the interviews may move into the domain of problems (What's wrong around here). The interviewer can choose to:

(a) Listen in the recognition that you won't get to the appreciative data until the problem is out, but don't expand the problem, listen for the moment to move on.
(b) Take note and come back to it later under a catch all question about what you would change if you could.
(c) Guide them back to the work of the interview.

The role of the observer

The role of the observer is to listen for the conditions for successful corporate working (that give the interviewee the feeling of success and vitality in their corporate role) that underpinned the interviewee's stories and make notes of these. The conditions need to be specific (saying good communication is not enough – what made it good, who was involved). Conditions might be things like:

- Being listened to.
- Focusing on something that mattered to us all.
- Enough time for planning.
- Discussing the context fully before a meeting.
- Involving stakeholder.

Your will then share your interpretations with the interviewer and interviewee at the end of the interview and come to some conclusions about the conditions that enabled the interviewee to work at their best.

These you bring to a dialogue with others that have been undertaking these interviews. Here you all map up the conditions and begin a whole group dialogue about conditions that foster success.

Resources

Cooperrider, D., Sorensen, P., Whitney, D. & Yaeger, T. (1999) *Appreciative Inquiry. Rethinking Human Organization Toward A Positive Theory of Change*. Stripes.

Annis-Hammond, S. (1998) *The Thin Book of Appreciative Inquiry* (Thin Book Series). Thin Book Publishing Company.

Positive difference and problem solving

- Dissipative systems

To move a system from aggressive opposition to active problem solving.

Small and large groups.

Working with difference can strike fear in our hearts as we remember the last time different views became personalised clashes of unremitting aggression. Difference or conflict becomes intense and emotionally charged. Resolving conflict for some can mean getting the opposition to come round to our point of view! In systems we know that to solve problems we need to work with different, multiple and conflicting views and ways of seeing the world. Difference is an asset not a liability. Groups naturally avoid conflict and thus dialogue, and leaders try to remove mess in organisations. Both of these conspire to dampen creativity. Meaning is created in conflict-laden decisions.

In working with complex problems where there will be multiple perspectives, where members of the system hold deeply embedded assumptions about other members' views, where the pattern has been to be subtlety or overtly aggressive with these differences. In designing practices for conflict we offer the following:

(a) Use dialogue as the core process but with the starting point being something symbolic that represents the person's engagement with the issue – what it means to them. So for instance ask all the individuals to share metaphors of their communities (their identity); ask them to draw their experience so far with the conflict issue. These are ways of doing what is identified in the dialogue practice as 'slowing down the inquiry'. Create the conditions for listening by shifting the focus of the conversation onto everyone's personal perception and identity.

(b) Again in a dialogue set-up, ask everyone to give a decent amount of time to the issue. Often in conflict situations, the group/system tries to deal with it too quickly, and ends up just persistently resurfacing the emotionally raw face of the conflict. We suggest spending a day on the issue, with time spent on ground rules; practice of dialogue; and then respectful listening as each party explains their perception at length, uninterrupted, and their hopes for the future. By polarising the conflict – pushing for the extremes in safe space with dedicated time, the group can reach new agreements.

(c) Margaret Wheatley has designed a five stage process for groups in conflict that uses different configurations of space to work through a model of understanding, focusing on intent and action.

I   Cooling – sitting in circle as individuals

II Enriching through fruitful opposition – sitting in a square with like-minded others.

III Magnetising resources – sitting in a half circle facing the unknown

IV Precise destroying – sitting in a triangle.

V   Intelligent action

We suggest that you read the full article of this process on the website http://www.margaretwheatley.com/articles/solvingnotattacking.html

Resources

Wheatley, M.J. & Crinean, G. (2004) Solving, not attacking, complex problems. a five-state approach based on an ancient practice. http://www.margaretwheatley.com/articles/solvingnotattacking.html

Positive deviance

Positive deviance was pioneered in response to childhood malnutrition in Vietnam. The US Save the Children officer Jerry Sternin knew that traditional solutions were not going to work here, and that the communities themselves had to find a way of beating malnutrition with no extra resources in order for the solution to be sustainable. He found that some children were well nourished in comparison to the majority, and these were from equally poor families. He then worked with the community to identify the conventional behaviours and beliefs about feeding children, and how the nourished children's feeding deviated from the community's norms.

"A positive deviant is one whose special practices or behaviours enables him/her to outperform or find better solution to a problem than his/her neighbour who has access to the same resources."

He found that there were specific differences (adding tiny shrimps and crabs from the paddy fields and greens from sweet potato tops to the child's diet; feeding the children 4/5 times a day rather than the traditional 2 times) and that these were behaviours that the neighbours could learn. The mothers came to a neighbour's house and learnt to cook the new food, and were supervised in feeding their children more regularly. The mothers were required to bring the new foods to the house, to cook it and to feed their children over a 2-week period, with regular weighing to see the impact it had on their child's weight. These new behaviours became normalised in that time and the mothers continued to feed their children in this way over time.

Positive deviance is based on the belief that every community has the answer within it to solve its own complex pervasive problems. There will be individuals in the community who are already finding their own way through the problem, by doing something different from the rest of the community. The individuals are called 'positive deviants'. The trick is to find these individuals and enable the community to learn these different behaviours across the whole.

The steps in the practice are these:

1. Define the problem, and what a successful outcome would look like.

2. Find out if there are individuals in the community already solving the problem (the positive deviants).

3. Uncover their behaviours and practices that enable them to succeed where their neighbours are not (find out the norms and how these positive deviants differ in their behaviour).

4. Show the new behaviour to neighbours and practice it together over a sustained period. Create a new habit. "It's easier to act your way into a new way of thinking than to think your way into a new way of acting".

Reference

Sternin J. (2003) Practice positive deviance for extraordinary social and organizational change. In: Ulrich, D., Goldsmith, M., Carter, L., Bolt, J. & Smallwood, N. (eds) *The Change Champions Fieldguide*. New York: Best Practice Publications.
www.bestpracticepublications.com

The end

Whilst this might be the end of this particular contribution to your thinking and practice, we hope it's the beginning of a different way of working for you. Many of the practices we have shared here are still evolving, particularly as we explore how to make them integral to daily organisational life. Most of our experience has been in using some of the practices designed for larger groups as a starting point for different conversations in the organisations we work with. We often get asked about impact.

What we are offering here is a different way of being together to work on and intervene in complex issues. The outcomes are often in improvements in relationships, and a different way of seeing 'what counts'. As these ideas haven't been part of organisational life (explicitly) for very long, there has been little research. There are some studies over recent years that can demonstrate improvement in outcomes (both in terms of staff satisfaction and clinical ones for a group of primary care practices in the USA), and some anecdotal evidence from leaders about the impact they are seeing (for instance the MD from the bank in our introductory story). The evaluation of the whole systems approach to primary health care development showed improved intra- and inter-agency relationships; stronger foundations for partnership working; increased user involvement and participation; and beneficial service change (Jee et al, 1999).

In taking these practices into your organisational life, we ask that you work with them and the principles underlying them as a collection, not take individual practices in isolation. In the section on design we offered a number of principles for design that go alongside the practices, that will help you shape your work. Here is a short story of where we have worked on design using multiple practices:

A local authority we worked with was locked into silo working. The departments were into preserving themselves and their own ways of working, with no concern for the knock-on effects on other departments, and little concern for the whole. As problems begun to mount up, each department blamed the way other departments worked. We started working with a design team that comprised eight people who volunteered/or were volunteered by the chief executive, from each of the departments. It was group of directors/senior managers. This group, whilst at least willing to work on how to get the LA working better together, still mirrored all the problems of working across departments. We worked with the design team to uncover their own patterns of behaviour, their own beliefs about 'togetherness', their own relationships in the room with us. This was the real time case material for the design of a two-day event for the whole organisation.

A number of principles emerged for the design that, on the face of it, looked obvious and very easy, but were at the core of the organisation's difficulties for instance: 'every one will have a voice so that all can participate'. Over 200 people came to a two-day event which incorporated appreciative interviewing across departments; developing guiding principles for the organisation as a collective; playing those principles out in mixed groups and in departments to explore what that would mean in terms of behaviours and actions; feedback between groups and departments (what the impact would be on them). At the end of the two days we had a review. In the discussion, people stood up and told their own stories of the event, with many touching on how their assumptions about other groups had changed, how they had been able to participate fully and have their voice heard, how they had learnt tools to use in their own groups.

Two months later we came back to explore, with anyone that wanted to turn up, how they were getting on. Again people told stories of using appreciative interviewing in their own groups, and when working on issues that required working across groups. Some of the listening techniques had been useful when the top team slipped back into battleground behaviour e.g. the talking stick as an aid to listening. Some had gone to shadow people in other parts of the organisation, to find out how they worked. There were many stories of renewed invigoration about working together. The design team debrief took them deeper in their dialogue into how they mirrored their part of the organisation and how they could develop their own leadership for the whole.

In working with these ideas in practice, we would be delighted if you can keep in touch with us, let us know if you refine any practices or have other ones to offer. We hope that we are contributing to a growing community interested in change in complex systems. We can only do that together.

References

Jee, M., Popay, J., Everitt, R. & Eversley, J. (1999) *Evaluation of a Whole Systems Approach to Primary Care Development*. London: King's Fund.

Index